D1368053

YOU

MEET

SUCH

INTERESTING

PEOPLE

By Bess Whitehead Scott

Texas A&M University Press

COLLEGE STATION

Copyright © 1989 by Bess Whitehead Scott
Manufactured in the United States of America
All rights reserved
First Edition

The paper used in this book meets the minimum requirements
of the American National Standard for Permanence of Paper
for Printed Library Materials, Z39.48-1984. Binding materials
have been chosen for durability.

Library of Congress Cataloging-in-Publication Data
Scott, Bess Whitehead, 1890–
    You meet such interesting people / by Bess Whitehead
Scott. — 1st ed.
        p.   cm. — (The Centennial series of the Association
of Former Students, Texas A&M University ; no. 33)
    Includes index.
    ISBN 0-89096-404-1 (alk. paper)
    1. Scott, Bess Whitehead,—1890– 2. Journalists—United
States—Biography. 3. Hearing impaired—United States—
Biography. 4. Scott, Bess Whitehead—Friends and
associates. 5. Texas—Social life and customs. I. Title.
II. Series.
PN4874.S36A3 1989
070'.92'4—dc19
[B]   88-30371
                                                           CIP

TO THE MEMORY OF MY MOTHER
Caroline Barnett Whitehead
AND MY SISTER
Elizabeth Whitehead Owen

It wasn't easy in 1915 for a woman to get her foot in the city room door. Bess Scott made it because she understood one of the basic principles of the newspaper business—everyone has a story. You have only to discover it and tell it well. . . .

She will tell you in this book about meeting interesting people, but you will also learn that there are few more interesting people than Bess Scott. The only thing better than reading the book is hearing Bess tell these stories herself. Enjoy.

WILLIAM P. HOBBY

Contents

Illustrations

Preface

Little did I dream in the quieter days of the early 1900s when I was determinedly seeking a place in the world of newspaper reporting that some day a record of these efforts and the subsequent seventy-five years in this profession might interest others. If this is the case, it is because I was a pioneer, working always on the "city side," a domain at that time considered sacred to men only. When I broke this taboo in 1915, I was the first woman in Houston to do so and one of the first in Texas.

This informal chronicle reflects highlights of ninety-seven years of living in an incredible age in which great nations have fallen from glory and lesser ones have gained in power. My part has been confined, of course, to a little corner of the world in my native Texas. I am writing about my colleagues and friends, looking back in astonishment at some of our experiences, with a deep appreciation and affection for all those who helped me over the rough places and enjoyed the small triumphs with me. Especially am I writing to all the women who aspire to this profession I love. I will not quote the many clichés that have become meaningless with overuse but will say from my heart what my college coach used to tell us in a voice choked with emotion: "You can do *anything* you want to if you want to *e-n-o-u-g-h!*"

In writing these memoirs I am, as I always was, a reporter—not an editor, not a columnist, not a critic or analyst. My long training as a reporter conditioned me to witness, describe, and quote rather than interpret, and, when writing interviews, to depict the personality and report the opinions of the person interviewed rather than my own opinions. Such factual reporting may seem dull to readers today who lean more to the sensational. Then why write of a life that has spanned decades of changed mores but cannot be called sensational? A friend has answered this: "There have been so many changes in the past century that a rural childhood in Texas nearly a hundred years ago has more in common with medieval yeomanry than with life in a small town anywhere in contemporary America. It is important to recover for the present and the future a past that is beyond recall except for those who actually experienced it." Readers may agree or not, but if they stay with me, I hope they will understand and be tolerant with my way of writing and the little sidelights memory brings that may sometimes seem unrelated to the subject at hand.

Background information on various historical events I obtained from the following sources: *The Art of American Films,* by Charles Higlaw; *Hollowell's Film Guide,* by Leslie Hollowell; *Mary Pickford and Douglas Fairbanks,* by Curtis Nunn; *Minutes of the 1916 State Convention,* compiled by the Texas Press Association; *Something about Brown: A History of Brown County Texas,* by T. R. Havins; and materials in the Texas Collection at Baylor University, courtesy Kent Keeth, director.

I am indebted to too many friends and associates who have helped me remember and write down these highlights of my life to record their names here. But I must mention my sainted older sister, Elizabeth Whitehead Owen, who taught me to read at the age of five and who through all the ninety-nine years of her life encouraged me to follow my bent—and write. Many of the family happenings told here are from her exceptional memory and occurred before I was born or when I was too young to remember them.

My thanks go also to my niece, Ruth Whitehead Chorlian, herself a published writer. My very special thanks go to Ellen Manion, without whose mechanical skill and generous help I would have given up in frustration. I also salute my practical and generous writer friend, Liz Carpenter, who paved my way to publication.

A friend I made many years ago is a noted novelist living in Cuernavaca, Mexico: Elizabeth de Trevino. She encouraged and inspired me to write this book. Also, a Houston friend, Lou Letts, prodded me for years to write about my experiences. She said, "Start this way: 'I was born in Blanket, Texas, twelve miles from Comanche.' That will sell a hundred books." (Finally did it, Lou and Elizabeth!)

These personal reports are largely from memory. If there are misquotes and wrong conclusions drawn, none was written in censure or bitterness. So, grant me the blessings of understanding and tolerance, and accept my sincere thanks for reminiscing with me.

YOU
MEET
SUCH
INTERESTING
PEOPLE

1.

The Whiteheads of Blanket

I was a birthday present to my mother, born on her thirty-fifth birthday, December 13, 1890. But since I was her ninth child, and came along when she had thought her childbearing days were over, she was not overjoyed with the present. It was not until I had children of my own and Mother lived with me that she told me she cried when I was born a girl.

"We had so many children and could do so little for them," she explained. "I felt boys could get along better than girls as they grew up. But Taz said he was tired of boys and that he was going to make a new cradle for you because you were a girl. That was typical of Taz. He said, 'Carrie, our little boys will grow up and marry and have homes of their own. This little girl will be with us a long time and be a joy to us in our old age, or a comfort to the one of us that is left.' He was right. It would have been hard for me to get along without you."

My father died with I was two. But, for the rest of her life, my mother was with me or near me.

My parents were Southerners. Sarah Caroline Barnett was born in 1855 on a cotton plantation near Rome, Georgia, into a large family of means; William Tazewell Whitehead, the youngest child of Cary Whitehead and Catherine Taliaferro Whitehead, was born on a tobacco plantation in Amherst County, Virginia, in 1845. Lured by reports of fertile virgin land farther south, Cary was inspired to move his family there and build a new life where cotton was king. Thus, in 1858, my grandparents, a middle-aged couple with grandchildren, pulled up their roots and resettled in northern Georgia. The men and slaves went by wagons and horseback. The women, white and black, went by train. Talk of the slaves being freed within a few years did not impress Cary.

"There will be slaves when little Taz here is an old man," Cary said. Taz, my father, was thirteen.

I regret that I did not know my grandmother Whitehead, always called "Callie." My mother knew her and told me she was a small, brunette woman, with great pride in her family heritage, and a superb horsewoman, "queen" of her household. "A gentlewoman in every sense of the word," Mother described her. She objected strongly to the move to Georgia and agreed only after Cary promised her he would build an exact duplicate of the home she was leaving in Virginia. This he did, in advance of their move. Callie insisted on the Italian pronunciation of her name Taliaferro instead of the English pronunciation of "Tolliver," but her kin who moved with her to Georgia were English in appearance, customs, and heritage. Mother knew many of them as "Tolliver."

How my father and mother met was an oft-told tale in my family. From his home in northern Georgia, young Taz followed his two older brothers into the Civil War. He participated in some of the most devastating battles, including Bull Run and Gettysburg. Captured by Northern troops at eighteen, he was offered freedom for signing the oath of allegiance to the North. He signed the oath and immediately rejoined the Southern army, as did many other Southern captives. When the war ended, he went directly home with two of my mother's brothers, whom he had met in the army. The three of them walked much of the way.

When they reached the Barnett place, Taz, still several miles from his home, stood at the front gate while his friends went inside to greet their family. Taz sighted a little girl in a big cherry tree and called to her, "Hello, little sweetheart! Everybody is getting a hug and a kiss but me. Come down and give me a kiss!" Little Carrie just climbed higher in the cherry tree.

Taz was twenty. Carrie was ten. Six years later they were married. During those next years, life in Georgia was not easy for them. They often talked of joining his brothers Ben and Dick, who had bought adjoining farms near Blanket, Texas. When Ben wanted to sell his 160 acres after his wife died, Taz bought the land. It was December of 1877 when the move was made.

Taz and Carrie had three children, Jesse ("Jess") five; Beatrice,

The Whitehead family in Rome, Georgia, December, 1876, one year before their move to Texas: William Tazewell ("Taz") Whitehead and Sarah Caroline ("Carrie") Barnett Whitehead, and their children, Roxie Beatrice, Elizabeth Olive, and Jesse ("Jess") Barnett

three; and Elizabeth, fifteen months. They went by train to Dallas, the end of the line, where Dick met them with his wagon and team. Father bought another wagon and team and loaded the few household things that had been sent by freight.

The 150-mile trek to Blanket started in a cold, rainy norther. There were no paved roads. Mud gummed up the wagon wheels, causing them to stop often. Five-year-old Jess punched mud out of the wheels with the men. He was so proud of the boots Father bought him in Dallas, the mud and cold did not bother him. A twelve-year-old Whitehead cousin also was along. It took the little caravan fourteen days to reach Blanket.

The family moved into the one-room log cabin that Ben had built. Jess and Tom slept in the wagon, Beatrice on a trundle bed, and Baby Elizabeth on a feather mattress put in a trunk.

During January of 1878, Father cut the logs from his own land, split the logs into shakes, and, with the help of his brother and neighbors, added a hall and second room to the log house. Also, according to custom, he built a kitchen separate from the house, connecting it with a "dog run." This was a typical country structure of the times. During the next ten years, two more rooms were added to the log house for six more children—Daisy, Charles, Ben, Larkin, Kirby, and me. When I was one we moved into the larger six-room "plank" house that Father and his neighbors had been building on a gentle slope across a little cane patch from our log house. It faced the Big Road, twelve miles from Comanche to the east, fifteen miles from Brownwood to the west.

I remember vividly every part of that six-room house; it had long porches front and back, connected by a big hall, a living room with fireplace, a parlor, dining room, a big kitchen with a fireplace, a long shed room for the four younger boys, and a smokehouse attached to the kitchen. Here I spent my childhood. Daisy had died at four. Beatrice married a few months after we moved into the new house. A year later there came the great tragedy that was to change our lives. My stalwart father, working in a wet norther to save our grain crop, contracted pneumonia (a disease for which there was no known cure in those days), and died. It was February 10, 1893. He was forty-seven years old.

Of course, I do not actually remember my father. But I see him often now, ninety-five years after his death, through the eyes of my mother and my sister Elizabeth. "He was very blond with deep blue eyes that twinkled with pride and love for his family," Elizabeth told me. "He was a gentle man, a man of natural wit. But he left the disciplining of us to Mother, never touched one of us in anger." Mother agreed. "Yes," she said, "When one of you misbehaved, he would say to me, 'Carrie, you ought to whip that child.' He wouldn't do it himself." That he was a great reader interested me. He read aloud to the family in the evenings, using a small Aladdin lamp to light the pages.

I think most children have a fear of talking about the dead. As a little girl I seldom asked about my father, but I treasured in my heart the picture of him as a kind, caring man. After I grew older,

I understood the times when I knew Mother was quietly weeping.

My brother Ben once told me one of his remembrances of Father. Ben was nine years old and seated at the family table with Charles, Larkin, and Kirby one Sunday when friends were having dinner with us. The men were talking of how rapidly Dallas was growing from the little village at the end of the rail line in 1877.

"I heard you were offered land there at that time for about a dollar an acre, Taz. Aren't you sorry you didn't take it? You might have been a millionaire in time," one of the men said teasingly.

"No," Father said unhesitatingly, "malaria and fever were rampant on that land along the river. If I'd stayed there, I might have lost one of my boys. Any one of them is worth a million dollars."

"Gee!" Ben remembered thinking, "I'm worth a million dollars to Pa!"

While my mother was confronted with raising a big family without a husband to help, the whole country was hit by one of the most devastating droughts in history. It was known as the "Cleveland Panic" because Grover Cleveland was U.S. president. On the Whitehead farm the corn crop was "nubbins"—little, stunted ears. The yield of cotton on forty acres of land was two bales and sold for six cents a pound. Mother and Jess, who at twenty had assumed the responsibility of the family with Mother, sold forty-six head of cattle for eighty-five dollars to buy feed to fatten the hogs, our only winter meat. They also managed to feed two work horses, two saddle horses, and six milk cows. Elizabeth, sixteen, and Charles, eleven, did the milking and cared for the cows.

They also strained the fresh milk and poured it into earthen jars, which were set in the cooler on the shaded back porch. Jess had made the cooler, a cage with wooden frame covered with screen wire. The bottom was a zinc trough about five inches deep, with a drainage pipe. The trough was kept filled with cool water. Legs held the cage waist high from the floor. Strips of two sacks made of loose fiber used to haul farm products were sewn around the jars and kept wet. The cooler was placed to catch breezes from the south and was a real boon in Texas' hot spring and summer months.

The milk was an important food for our growing family, along with the butter churned from the rich cream that was left to turn slightly sour. The clabber, left when the cream was skimmed off, was relished, as was the buttermilk that remained after butter was churned from the cream.

Every member of the family had a milk preference. As the youngest, I was given sweet milk (fresh milk) and was often privileged to skim a little of the sweet cream off a jar! I am reminded of an incident that occurred fifty years later when I was in New York. Early in the morning while my tour companions were still sleeping, I walked to a nearby sidewalk cafeteria and ordered a doughnut, coffee, and a glass of sweet milk. The waitress looked puzzled and asked hesitantly, "Lady, what is *sweet* milk?" Then I was puzzled. "You know what buttermilk is, don't you?" She nodded. "Well," I said, "I don't want sour buttermilk. I want sweet milk." "Oh," she said brightly, "you mean *white* milk!" We were raised in different worlds.

In spite of hardships and flat purses, our growing family ate well. My brothers gathered the wild plums and wild grapes that covered our creek banks and pasture fences in the fall and helped wash and stem them to be canned or preserved for winter. They also picked peaches from our orchard and Uncle Dick's and cleaned and cut them to dry in the sun on tarpaulins and sheets stretched on the roof of the house. These dried fruits showed up later in fried pies for our school lunches.

When she was ninety-seven, Elizabeth told me of the hardships of the Cleveland Panic years. "Mother had steeled herself with an indomitable will and courage to face the reality of caring for us and making ends meet. But her strength was not to endure. Three months after Father's death, she was stricken with a severe case of sciatica and was in bed for several weeks." From her bed she taught the little boys to make their own beds and help Elizabeth with all the house and kitchen chores. I was nearly three years old. Elizabeth became my second mother.

The panic years, which had hit all farmers alike, passed and life resumed a more normal routine. The boys all started to school and helped with farm work as well; and I grew from babyhood during these years.

My mother's belief was that honest work and accepting responsibility as a family member strengthened character. Bless her memory! I know she was right. So I was sent to the woodpile daily to fill a small basket with chips and bring it to the woodbox by the kitchen stove. I was proud of my job and rejoiced that I was "as big as Kirby." Actually, he was three years older. But I was not allowed to go into the horse lot to pick up the corn cobs for fuel, as he was. This was a cross for me to bear and often a cause for the quarrels between us in which I was usually the loser. I'm sure I provoked many of the little set-to's, often taking the roughing because I hated to be called a "crybaby." Much later, I understood that Kirby probably resented me because at three years he was robbed of his "baby" status, and by a girl at that. *¡Pobrecito!*

Another daily job that I really enjoyed was sitting on a stool near Mother and "tacking" carpet rags. Most of the floors in those days were covered with woven carpets. The best parts of sheets, flour sacks, and clothing were washed and dyed bright colors. These were ripped into long strands about one inch wide. The strands were tucked together by hand, end to end, with strong sewing thread, then wound into balls. When enough balls were finished to make a carpet of the desired size, they were taken to the home of a neighbor, who wove the carpet on her huge loom. They were similar to the braided rugs popular today. I stood in awe of the big loom and was fascinated at the way she handled it. I was also fascinated with the many magazines stacked in the corner of a room of her house that was a step below the other floors. I managed to sit on the floor there, quietly absorbed in the stacks of pictures and reading matter I never found anywhere else. The quiet hours I spent tacking the balls for the carpets are treasured memories. I felt secure and loved as Mother sat nearby mending clothes or sewing on her machine instead of being occupied with household duties in the kitchen or yard. She always broke my working hour by giving me milk or lemonade and allowed some moments for play. But she saw to it that I did the work assigned. If I did a sloppy job, I had to do it over.

Another and harder job was mine when I reached eight years. To serve all our needs, we had ten coal oil lamps, all with chimneys and some decorated with colorful designs. On Saturday mornings under Mother's supervision I took the lamps one by one, emptied the coal oil, washed the lamps in soap suds, and rinsed and dried them to sparkling perfection. As I finished each one, I placed it on the kitchen fireplace mantel. Mother would not let me fill them again with the coal oil, but when she said, "They are real pretty, Bessie," I was satisfied. She had a sharp tongue for my older sisters if they smoked my bright chimneys with their curling irons. The culprit had to clean them.

My brothers spent many evening hours in sand-lot baseball games, fishing, and swimming in the cattle tank, and at mysterious gatherings with neighbor boys by camp fires along Blanket Creek, which turned out to be "chicken roasts." I was never welcomed at any of these forays and felt ignored and abused. Mother worried about these campfire parties and about the neighbors whose chickens turned up missing. "We've got plenty of chickens," she would say. "I'd give the boys all they want. They don't have to steal them!" But Jess, probably wishing he were young enough to join the fun, would say, "Let 'em alone, Ma. They are better off at this than a lot of other things."

"Fire Ball" was another game I could not join. It was a Saturday night game as a rule. The boys saved every bit of twine throughout the week and made the pieces into balls, which they soaked in coal oil. At dark on Saturday they set fire to the balls and played a running game of pitch as long as the burning balls lasted. Any boy who tried to wear gloves was a sissy. Mother made them play in Uncle Dick's field, which was across the Big Road from our house. I had to stay in our yard and watch from afar. Often Jess would sit on the high front porch with me, as a spectator. Running after fireflies was a diversion for me while I waited for the game to end and for the players to race each other back to the house. Mother or Elizabeth usually had buckets of lemonade ready that I could share with the boys. I do not know why, but it seems to me everybody had nicknames in those days. My brothers were Shooter, Clip, Eages, and Snooks. Jesse was "Jess" to everybody all his life. Beatrice was "Bea," or "Sister," and Elizabeth was always "Lizzie." I was "Bessie," which was my real name.

In time, Charles and Ben grew to dating age and left the fire balls to Larkin and Kirby and their friends. Charles and Ben were popular

Jess Whitehead, Sarah Caroline Whitehead, and "Sister" (Beatrice), Blanket, Texas, 1950

teenagers, and Elizabeth and her friends and my sister Beatrice and her husband, Atison Gray, joined other young couples in the area for square dancing and games. There were always plenty of talented guitar, mandolin, and fiddle players, and these festive Saturday night parties lasted as long as the farm parents would allow. Mother always wanted them to be at our house, where she could keep an eye on *her* girls. No trouble was too much for her to take to keep her herd at home and to see that they had a happy, and in her eyes, morally acceptable good time. To her credit, the Whitehead "Do-Si-Do's" were popular for miles around.

I was as excited as anybody before and during those parties, although I often fell asleep and was carried to bed in the early evening hours. I had a finger in all the getting ready when the boys moved furniture out of the two front rooms and prepared extra lamps and even porch lanterns. I appointed myself as the official taster of the ambrosia punch, homemade ice cream, and pies and cakes—so long as Mother permitted.

I remember one occasion when Larkin, who was a good dancer, wanted to take up the carpet and all the straw padding under it because he couldn't dance the Cotton-Eyed Joe on the carpet. When Mother refused, Larkin sulked and I cried, as I always did when any of my brothers was unhappy. For once, Larkin accepted my sympathy. He and I sat on the back porch steps, where he put his arm around me, and we fussed about the "old fogey old folks." I was eight, Larkin was fourteen. I felt as old as he was!

I recall, with reason, another of our at-home soirées. A popular game of the times was charades. Scenes from a play or song, or imitations of persons were presented in silhouette by groups or a single actor. Onlookers wrote down their guesses of the subject or theme presented. The person correctly guessing the most themes won a prize.

The first scene that night was of a popular Blanket girl named Maude, poised with a rake and a scattering of hay. Maude Mueller "in the meadow sweet with hay" was easily guessed. Then I came in wearing a red crocheted hood carrying a basket on my arm. The applause for "Little Red Ridinghood" was meant to please me, and everybody was shocked when I began to cry loudly and call for "Mama." I had tasted too generously of the ambrosia in advance of the party; stomachache and nausea were the Big Bad Wolf after me that night.

The dances, the songs, and the loud voice of the caller all fascinated me, and I longed for the day when I could take part. Alas! By the time I reached the square dance age, we had left the farm and were out of the Do-Si-Do area. I never learned to square dance, but many of the tunes and words remain with me, and I still can see the laughing dancers.

> Shoot the Buffalo,
> Shoot the Buffalo,
> Ramble through the canebrakes,
> And shoot the Buffalo!

> One wheel off the little red wagon,
> One wheel off the little red wagon,
> One wheel off the little red wagon,
>   You're the one, my darling!

Atison Gray, Beatrice's husband, was a natural musician who could play many instruments by ear and had a good voice. Since this sister never had children of her own, she often had me live at their farm for a week or more at a time. Atison would make up songs and sing to me accompanied by his mandolin. Or he would jog me on one knee as he sang—

> Heigh, Ho, Bessie-O!
> How in the devil
> Do the old folks know
> Bessie loves sugar
> In her coffee-o!

2.

Mother and Elizabeth

During my first eight years, my heart broke every weekday morning when my brothers walked down the Big Road on their way to school two miles away. I could not go. A serious ear infection that started in babyhood kept me at home except for a month or so in the fall and in the spring. Brown County had colder weather then than now, and snow fell often in the winter. If I got out even for a half hour of play with my big dog Pup, I was well bundled up and wore close-knit wool hoods that my mother and sister made. I had red or dark blue for every day, pink and blue or white for Sunday.

I learned to play alone for hours. My dolls and their furniture and cradles that I made from boxes comforted me. I made a piano of the big removable top to Mother's sewing machine and sang Sunday-school songs while I played spiritedly on the "piano." I sang the words as I heard them, often inaccurately. When I sang, "At the Cross—where I received my sight" it came out "Ira ceived my sight." I thought the song was about Ira Russell, who lived in Blanket! Mother made a "lob-lobby" place under the grape arbor near our well and let me play "mud pies" and serve them to my dolls. My treehouse was a limb in the big mesquite tree in our front yard, which also became my horse or my bicycle, according to my mood. Pup, the ferocious-looking half-bull mutt, was my constant companion.

One of my greatest joys was reading, or pretending to read, the few newspapers, magazines, and books that were available in our home. These were, for the most part, books Elizabeth had purchased for the few college semesters she could finance. She taught me to read when I was five, and although Shakespeare was beyond me, I would "read" the pictures, lying flat on my stomach with the heavy volumes spread out on the floor. Milton's *Paradise Lost,* a huge book with beautiful pictures in color, fascinated and scared me. If I asked her, Elizabeth would tell me the stories. Later, when I played alone, I would tell my dolls the stories in my own words. My mother, always practical and compelled by circumstances to be tough, was not a reader. She strictly forbade her children to read trash, and any paperback was trash to her. She frowned on the popular comic book of that day, "Peck's Bad Boy," but Kirby and I loved it. As I grew older, no rule against reading could stop me. I hid *Three Weeks* and *Tempest and Sunshine* on the top of our big privy under the plum tree in our orchard and read them until Mother's fretful call returned me to the house. Of our younger family, only Kirby and I were readers. Kirby had to do field work with the older boys the year round and seldom had time to read. In sympathy, Elizabeth shared her books as much as she could. Kirby and I squabbled over them and the *Youth's Companion,* the only magazine we received, but when Kirby was at school, or in the fields in the summer, I had the book world to myself. When I was six, I told Elizabeth, then twenty, "I'm going to write my own 'Peck's Bad Boy' when I grow up." Always supportive, she assured me that I would.

I only had one picture book that I remember, and I can see and repeat my favorite page even now. The picture was of a little sailor boy leaning on a tree by a little stream, his sailor hat with blue ribbons lying on the grass. The verse read:

> Little boy, little boy, why
>   do you dream
> Sitting alone on the banks
>   of the stream?
> "I'm waiting," said he
>   'til the stream has gone by.
> I'm thinking of crossing as
>   soon as 'tis dry.

I loved verses and poems, and although I did not know the meaning of the words much of the time I loved the rhythm, which I tried to imitate.

One effort remains in memory. I was sitting on my "horse" in the mesquite tree and saw our country doctor go by in his buggy. I wrote in the style of my picture book, as I held my doll:

Little doll, little doll, why
   do you stare
Down the Big Road from
   up in the air?
"I'm looking," said she,
   "for old Doctor Cobb,
He'd better come quick or he'll
   lose his job."

"Is that a poem?" I asked Elizabeth.

"Well," she said, "it is a parody."

"What's a parody?"

She got the big dictionary and helped me look it up. I wrote it down in the back of my picture book and never forgot it.

Through my childhood and teen years, I tried to write—verse, essays, and love stories. I kept these hidden in a shoebox but occasionally allowed Elizabeth to read and criticize them. After she married and moved away, I sometimes sent her my efforts. She always considered them seriously, even the sentimental (and hilarious) love stories of my "Aurora" heroine. She pointed out errors or praised without flattery. She later helped me in my professional writing and in spirit is helping me now.

Elizabeth encouraged my reading at all ages, but she also urged me to play outside. In fact, when I was still too young to walk alone down the Big Road to the Knudsons' farm, she would walk me there, return home, and two hours later come back to walk me home. This allowed me to play with Carrie and her sisters in the playhouse their father had made in a clump of small oaks in their backyard. Smooth wire stretched around the trees set off rooms of the house. We made furniture out of cardboard boxes and made aprons from tree leaves "sewed" together with brittle stems of broomweeds. Mrs. Knudson served us sandwiches of cold biscuits, home-cured bacon, and sweet onions from her garden. Milk was our "coffee."

I was never ready to go home when Elizabeth came for me, but knew I had to go. "We'll soon have to start the feeding and milking and all the evening work," she would remind me. "We mustn't be late or Ma might have a switch out!" So we would walk the quarter mile home as she had me listen to an occasional bobwhite whistle or note the wild flowers or maybe the first fruit on our orchard trees. The walks were almost as much fun as the playhouse.

I remember one of these walks in late December as an important turning point in my life. I hesitantly asked Elizabeth, "Is there a real Santa Claus? Callie said you and Mama are my Santa Claus."

Callie was Carrie's older sister. As we sat on the steps eating our sandwiches that afternoon, she had said, "You know there's no real Santa Claus, don't you? Your mama puts your Christmas gifts in your stockings and on the mantel." I was stunned, but not for the world would I let Callie see that.

"Of course I know that." I'm sure my voice showed Callie I was fibbing. I had a heavy heart and was glad it was near time for Elizabeth to come after me.

We walked in silence for a time after I had questioned Elizabeth. Then she quietly reminded me of the Christmas story and told me how legends of Santa had grown up in many countries, that Santa Claus, under different names, stood for the spirit of giving and sharing and the joy that Jesus' birth brought to the world. I was satisfied.

It was a year after this that Elizabeth talked to me of her belief in Christ as a personal savior and the real meaning of my Sunday-school lessons. She did not talk down to me but told me what it meant to her to be a believer. I wanted to be a Christian too. With the encouragement of Mother and my sisters, I joined the Blanket Baptist Church. I was nine years old. My faith has endured.

If I have pictured my practical mother as a harsh taskmaster and a woman unsympathetic to her children's needs and dreams, nothing could be more unfair. At a very early age I recognized her as my closest companion and my security. Intuitively, I knew of the great tenderness of her love for me. As we grew in years, our knowledge of her loyalty and her profound longing for our success and happiness also grew. She found this hard to say in words, but she continually expressed it in deeds. She was uncompromising in her convictions of right and wrong, and she taught us that we must accept the consequences of our mistakes. But she was understanding and compassionate and suffered deeply when her children suffered. She cleared a shining path for us to follow, and to the end of her ninety-six years we revered her as our mentor and guide. I might have made

The author's mother, Sarah Caroline Whitehead, Brownwood, Texas, 1895

it without her, but the burden would have been terrific. I could never have done my work as well without the comforting knowledge my children were well cared for and I had a haven where love abided.

My mother was born into a large and prosperous Georgia plantation family in late 1855 and was reared in the comfort of a large home, where slaves did the drudgery. Even after the Civil War and the hardships that followed the family's experience with Sherman's soldiers as they marched to the sea, after the loss of money and prop-

The author's sister, Elizabeth Whitehead Owen, Orofino, Idaho, 1974

erty, Mother was sent to a private girls' school and reared as a "Southern lady." Her father's death and the unsettled social and economic conditions helped push her into marriage at sixteen. She had three children by the time she was twenty-one and six more by her thirty-fifth birthday.

Not once in the sixty-five years I shared with my mother did she express regret at having left her sheltered world of gentle upbringing to follow my father to an alien land and hard years of near poverty. She worked beside her beloved "Taz" to make a home for us. After my father's sudden death in 1893, she told the children who were old enough to understand, "You stand by me, and I will always stand by you." She did. A comely young widow of thirty-five with the black hair and violet eyes of her Scotch-Irish mother, she refused offers of marriage and with her children successfully worked the small farm that held her family together.

Mother was seriously ill only once in her life, was never in a hospital, bore nine children, did the scrub-board and outdoor pot-boiling of the family laundry, made her own soap, baked her own bread, and fed her family from the produce of her land. A small woman, she ruled her five sons and four daughters with a kind but firm hand, showing them by example what a Christian life meant. She was selfless and devoted, a firm but loving disciplinarian, a loyal and always forgiving friend. At the age of ninety-six and a half, she died peacefully in her bed.

I do not have the words to tell what my mother meant to me, her "baby." More than sixty years after my marriage, I still have a deep feeling of guilt and regret that in 1918, carried away by the keyed-up days of World War I, by the unhappy ending of a longtime love dream, and by the charm and persistence of a childhood beau, I married while my mother was far away in Washington state visiting my sister. She wrote me a letter of bitter hurt, still trying hard to wish me happiness. I tore it up and spent one of the tear-filled nights of my life. She feared, with reason, for my future happiness.

My mother-in-law, "Aunt Kate" Scott, had a whimsical expression of endearment for her children: "I couldn't make a living without you." Truly, I could never have made a living free of worry without my mother. She has a special place in this record of my work.

3.

Childhood Memories

From the time of my father's death when I was two years old, I slept with my mother on the big feather bed in our "fireplace room." That was our living room, where our family gathered after supper and talked or played games. The boys picked out pecans with their pocket-knives and joked or argued until bedtime. In the winter, the fireplace warmth was the center of activities, while breezes from the south windows made the summer nights pleasant.

Since I was partially deaf, I could not always join in the talk and laughter. I sat on a stool by Mother's knee, and when I did not understand the laughter I would say, "What is it, Mama?" One of the boys was apt to say, "Aw, it was nothing, Bessie." But with infinite patience Mother would always explain. Some things that I was able to hear and understand when the grown folks talked stay in my memory even now. For example, an edition of the Blanket newspaper ran an item about a costume party at Mrs. John Tucker's home, and the piece was read aloud while we all sat around the fireplace in the evening: "Among the happy guests were Miss Lizzie Whitehead . . . and Jess Whitehead. . . ." I was jealous when Elizabeth showed too much attention to others or too much attention was shown to her. I watched for my chance, and when the newspaper was left on the table, I stared to throw it on the flames in the fireplace.

"Oh no, let's not do that," Ben cautioned as he grabbed my arm.

"Mama!" I started to protest.

"Get into your nightgown," she interrupted me sternly. "You're going to bed."

Another evening around our fireplace, Jess, who listened a lot but seldom said much, was telling about a man who shut his neighbors' guineas up in his cellar because they pecked his watermelons. Everybody laughed at the absurdity of shutting the noisy birds in a cellar, and, as usual, I inquired, "What is it, Mama?" She explained and told me guineas said "pot-rack, pot-rack." I had never seen a guinea.

Other stories I only half understood but well remember were told with laughter about a neighbor woman who hollowed out the ends of her firewood and filled them with gunpowder to discourage thieves; how two well-known women, irked because their husbands lingered too long over a croquet game, broke up the game and used the croquet mallets to drive the men home to dinners that were getting cold; about the little McLaughlin boy who prayed: "Lord, Dad wants me to ride in the rodeo. I know I'll be pitched off. Please let me fall in a soft place." I sympathized with that little boy, but I did not understand why Mother didn't like the story of what one woman said to another about a new resident: "We have to be careful about this new woman—her dress is so short you can see her ankles!"

As a child, I was quick to absorb news and gossip as I understood them, and I enjoyed all the Blanket community affairs that I could attend with my family, such as Christmas Tree celebrations held alternately in the four Protestant churches in Blanket, Friday afternoon school "exhibitions," and "protracted meetings" at the town arbor. The last, now called revival meetings, were often sponsored by two or more churches and drew crowds from many other towns in the area. Every summer, the arbor was renewed with a fresh tree-branch ceiling and a carpet of clean straw on the dirt floor. Many a small child was sent to nap on pallets laid over the thick straw. The benches were wide and long, with no backs. Before the services started, laughing boys and girls vied with each other, jumping from one bench to another, using the whole area as a race track. Special singing of well-known gospel songs opened the services, and as the intensity of the preacher's message grew, happy God's children mingled with the converts, dancing up and down the aisles, waving palm-leaf fans and praising the Lord. These were emotional occasions where people bared their souls without embarrassment and in pure joy. Mother, Elizabeth, and Beatrice attended these meetings, often with the Knudson neighbors. Although they were as devout as their friends and doubtless were emotionally moved, they worshiped more quietly. When tears sometimes dampened my tenderhearted sister Beatrice's cheeks, I was distressed and wiped them off with my mother's handkerchief. Sister would cuddle me, and when she patted my cheek,

I was reassured. Such incidents as these were impressed on me because they affected my beloved family even though I did not understand why. They left vivid memories.

At another of the revivals, Uncle Bunch Simpson "got religion." After a welcome by the minister, and much singing, Uncle Bunch was asked to lead a prayer of thanksgiving. He knelt at the altar as silence fell. Everyone knew Uncle Bunch as a hardened sinner and wondered what he would say. Silence . . . continued silence. Finally, Uncle Bunch raised his head.

"Preacher," he said, "I just can't cut 'er!"

Equal to the occasion, the minister raised his arms to stop the smothered laughter.

"Brother Simpson, it's all right. The Lord hears your heart! Let's sing 'Praise Him, Praise Him.'" I was dismayed. "Mama, why did they laugh at Uncle Bunch? They made him cry!"

"Hush, Bessie, sing with us now." I sang lustily, even as I told myself grown folks are funny.

In 1897, our church was sponsor of the Community Christmas Tree. Jess and Elizabeth drove our buggy through snow to help decorate the church that afternoon and stayed with friends until it was time for the program. Ben and Charles were with friends also and had ridden their saddle horses "downtown." Larkin and Kirby were to ride double on the remaining saddle horse in time for the festivities. As usual, I could not go out in winter snow because of my ear infection, and Mother and I had planned an evening of Christmas stories and popcorn made over our fireplace flames.

Larkin had gone to the lot to saddle Old Sol, and Kirby was to get on behind him as he rode out the gate to the Big Road. I was drawing pictures on the frosted windowpane when I saw Larkin ride out through the gate, turn right, and spur his horse into a lively gallop.

"Mama, Mama," I cried, "Larkin is leaving Kirby!" Mother and Kirby rushed to the front door. It was too late. Larkin was too far down the road to even hear them call. I cried loudly for Kirby, heartbroken for him. Mother was angered and grieved. Kirby stoically walked to the fireplace, not speaking. A big boy of twelve, he was not going to let anybody see him cry. He would not pop corn with us. He would not listen to Mother read the Christmas story or sing a carol with us. The new *Youth's Companion* magazine he loved lay untouched. Without speaking, he simply went to the room the four boys shared and went to bed. When Mother took him a cup of chocolate and cookies, he pretended to be asleep. "He's not sleeping in his and Larkin's bed," Mother told me as she returned to the fireplace and gave me the chocolate. "He's in Ben's bed. I don't blame him." I knew by her set mouth there would come a reckoning.

Next morning, Christmas Day, was one of the few days the family slept late. But Mother was up betimes. She had a purpose. Larkin at fourteen had grown to a six-foot sapling and towered over Mother. Knowing that she could not handle him if he chose to defy her, she had planned her strategy. Armed with a buggy whip, she pulled the covers back and applied the whip to the sleeping Larkin in the place that hurt the most.

Years later, Larkin, holding one of his own little boys on his lap, recalled the incident. "Ma sure poured it on," he remembered. "I knew I had it coming and just took it. I think she was sorry afterwards that she whipped me so hard. I was literally blistered by that buggy whip." I don't imagine Kirby was sorry.

The Blanket area was my whole world during the first sixteen years of my life. Our big farm family was typical of the 1880s and 1890s. Our life-style, work, and pleasures were those of our neighbors, and sibling jealousies and minor quarrels were common, just as they are today. One history of Brown County names fifteen families as pioneers of the region, including the Tazewell and Dick Whitehead families.

But Blanket's colorful history went back to 1873, when a small settlement was founded at a spot three miles south of the present town. Courageous pioneers led by Pinkney Anderson built the way station in line with the cattle trails winding over Texas to a market shipping point at Fort Worth and called it Blanket. The settlers built a merchandise store, a livery stable, and a blacksmith shop. When Mr. Anderson applied to the government for a post office, it was approved, and he was made postmaster. The first settlers were harassed by the Comanches and by wild animals, including wild hogs that sometimes attacked children. My family, like others, was proud of this heritage, and I often heard tales of those early days that worried me. When I asked questions, my brother Kirby was apt to tell me that the Indians and the wild hogs still lurked around the creek near us. Mother would scold him and warn me that Kirby was teasing. "Bessie, that was a long time ago before you were born," she would assure me. She never knew how my heart sometimes raced and how I ran fast when I had to cross the creek.

In early 1891, the Frisco Railroad extending from Fort Worth to Brownwood bypassed Blanket. Anderson and his neighbors solved this problem by moving the whole town to its present site, on the railroad. The town for some time was known as "New Blanket." The area was then in Comanche County, but when Mills County was created, the new survey put Blanket in Brown County.

Soon Blanket was a town of five hundred inhabitants, with grocery stores, meat markets, banks, barbershops, blacksmith shops, and all the other necessary businesses for a growing community. Five churches and better schools were founded, and two resident physicians and three lodges and their auxiliaries were in full swing in the next decade. In the years that I remember best, 1896 to 1907, Blanket was a thriving town, surrounded by prosperous farms and ranches, with an area population of twelve to fifteen hundred.

One of my most vivid remembrances is of the water well bored in the center of Main Street, where a windmill kept a long tank filled with fresh water for teams and saddle horses. A half-day's journey to the east was Comanche, and to the west, Brownwood, our nearest "cities." When the crops were harvested and money was in hand, families drove there in wagons for barrels of flour, sugar, molasses, and other staples.

Blanket suffered again when the paved state highway was built and only skirted the little town, buses taking the place of the railroad. But the local residents met the challenge. A citizens' committee was formed to plan improvements and encourage local marketing instead of the half-day drives by wagon or buggy to Comanche or Brownwood. Area roads were improved. A vacant building was turned into an attractive civic center for meetings, youth activities, and programs. In time, the long-proposed expansion of the school curriculum was achieved and new teachers were hired.

Today, Blanket still has a place in rural Texas as a town whose origin dates from the time when furrows were turned by walking plows drawn by horses or mules, planting was done by hand, cotton was picked by hand, grain was cut and stacked by hand, and each child was assigned chores in that daily routine of living.

Several stories have been told about how Blanket got its name — all "guess" tales. The most popular one is that before a town was there the Indians found the site on the creek to be an excellent camping place. They hung their colorful blankets on the sumac bushes, and the site was called the "blanket place." This story probably originated like the old joke still told in those parts: "Why are Comanche and Brownwood always cold? Because they have only one Blanket between them.

A more believable story is told by T. C. Smith, Jr. He wrote that a Frenchman, who was in the Blanket area long before there were any towns, was named Blanchtier. His camp was on the creek, so when a little settlement was established there, it was named "Blanket," an anglicized version of his name. Early Blanket settlers were law-abiding, God-fearing people, stoically accepting the good years of harvest and the bad years of drought, raising large families, content with simple pleasures. Their educational opportunities were limited but adequate for their needs. Other small towns that sprang up in the area and are still thriving are Cross Cut, Zephyr, May, and Indian Creek, the birthplace of author Katherine Anne Porter.

These communities experienced much the same joys and tragedies as our present crowded, clamorous world. Only in extent and proportion did they differ. Because the residents were fewer and "everybody knew everybody," the impact of events was greater, often devastating to the individuals and the community alike. Children in those days were more affected because of the closeness of family and friends. A few such experiences in the 1890s burned themselves into my mind in a way that brought me troubled dreams. Mother would not discuss them or answer questions, so I bottled them up in my mind, a source of anxiety and sometimes fear that I still remember.

One such event was the tragedy of a fifteen-year-old orphaned girl who was living with her aunt and uncle and of a teenage boy who was a member of a pioneer Blanket family. "Minnie" was a large, heavy girl, a newcomer who knew few of her Blanket schoolmates. The attentions of "Gene" were a balm to her loneliness. She became pregnant, but her size and loose clothing hid her condition even from her aunt. She gave birth to a premature baby one night while the sixteen-year-old father stood outside her window trying to comfort her. Whether by design or from panic—it was never determined— Minnie smothered the child between her mattresses. The county court was persuaded to take no action, but the friendship of the two families was destroyed. A pall hung over our school, felt from the youngest to the oldest, that has remained in my mind and heart for over eighty years.

In another tragedy, the son of a well-known Blanket family was shot to death by a young husband while he tried to hide under a table at the husband's home. The picture of this man trying to escape these bullets was etched into my young mind. I did not understand the tragedy, but for weeks the murder was a haunting nightmare.

Child molestation was a term never used in my childhood, but I experienced it in a mild way, another memory I will carry to my grave. A neighbor boy who was driving his wagon to Brownwood passed our farm and gave me a ride to Sister Beatrice's home west of Blanket on the road to Brownwood. As I sat on the wagon seat beside him, I suddenly felt his hand trying to go under my short dress. I held my skirt down firmly with both hands, and when we reached Blanket he let me alone. When I told Mother about it later, she said, "Bessie, try to forget this and don't ever tell anybody about it. Promise me." I didn't understand, but Mother's face and tone sealed my lips. I never told it, but I never forgot it either.

With happier thoughts, I remember when the 1902 Christmas tree was put up at the Baptist Church where my family worshiped. Veda Earp, daughter of the pastor and one of my chums, and I sang a duet we had written. I wrote the lyrics and she wrote the music. She also played the foot-pumped organ for everybody to sing carols. Summer "Singing Schools" were also highlights of those days around 1900. I'll never forget the name of the teacher who taught them. Tillet Teddley was from Fort Worth. Sometimes his brother came with him. He taught us the musical staffs, notes, the different tones —soprano, alto, tenor, and bass—and harmony. We kept notebooks.

I am indebted to him and the Singing Schools for being able to read musical notes and pick out melodies and for those happy hours that lightened the boredom of summer.

Veda was a beloved playmate and, with Carrie Knudson, we made a happy trio in many activities. One summer day when Veda and Carrie were both at my house on the farm we went out on the back porch just in time to see a chicken hawk light in an oak tree a few yards away.

"He'll get your chickens," Carrie warned. "My brothers shoot them." That gave me an idea. "We do too," I said. Veda, a town girl, asked why. "Because hawks eat chickens," Carrie explained. "I'll show you," I offered, and tried to pick up the big shotgun leaning in the corner of the porch. I had been warned never to touch the gun, but I was showing off. I dragged the gun to where I could brace it on a porch post. Before it was far enough off the porch to aim, I pulled the trigger.

"Bang!" went the kicking gun and the hawk flew away, no doubt laughing. Two frightened little girls were trying to raise me up off the floor just as Mother and Elizabeth came running. "I told the boys never to leave that gun on the porch!" scolded Mother. "You girls come into the kitchen and get some hot lightbread and butter." A trio of subdued little girls settled on the bench behind the big table, and Mother gave us freshly baked bread and big glasses of milk. I was especially quiet. I knew if Veda and Carrie had not been there my legs would have been tingling with a switching.

Another unforgettable experience was being too near a fight between Professor McDonald, principal of the Blanket school, and a student named Jim. It was noontime and all the girls except Carrie and me had taken their sack lunches outside on the school grounds. She and I went to one of the desks to eat. The trouble started outside. Jim drew a knife, and the unarmed teacher retreated backward into the big downstairs room. The older boys shoved the desks back and made a path from the front door to Professor McDonald's desk. Jim began to close in on the teacher. As he neared the potbellied stove, Mr. McDonald saw his chance. He grabbed the heavy iron poker and knocked the knife out of Jim's hand and floored him.

At that moment, Jim's mother rushed in, wearing a sunbonnet

and her kitchen apron. She took Jim in charge and marched him away, telling Professor McDonald that he would "pay for this."

Carrie and I jumped down from the wall desk to which we had retreated, just as all the students outside came in. It was a tense moment when we thought Jim was going to knife the teacher. The boy had a reputation for violence, and we expected somebody to get badly hurt. When the case came to trial in the county court, Carrie and I had to testify. Professor McDonald was exonerated. Jim, a minor, was released.

In this same term another school crisis ended in tragedy. Alice, one of the older girls, and I were caught in this, too, simply because we were there. The boys at recess were playing Pop the Whip, a favorite game where they joined hands, from smallest to largest. The big leader led the line to a fast pace, then turned swiftly and tried to pop the boys on the other end off the line. A close friend of my brother Ben was head of the line. Henry, a chubby little boy of ten, was on the other end. The big boys did pop Henry off the line. Usually this led to a harmless roll in the dirt. But Henry's head hit a big rock that no one had noticed, and the blow killed him.

Alice and I witnessed the accident. This time, the Blanket justice of the peace took statements from Alice and me and did not call us to testify. The court judged the affair an accident, blaming no one. But again the longtime friendship of two families was destroyed. My brother Ben told me years later that his friend never in his life felt entirely free from blame.

Despite some unpleasant incidents, my school years were happy ones. Kirby and I both brought a little honor to our family. This crusty brother, so hard to get along with, was a boy of unusual intelligence. He wrote and delivered an essay that won him a medal. Still in the elementary school, I won a medal in spelling. I was especially proud of it because I competed with all grades in the school, elementary through ninth. Principal McDonald taught the class and required that we memorize every part of the words in our spelling book, even "the" and "a."

We met at 1:00 P.M., all students gathering after the noon recess in the high-school auditorium. We lined up along three walls. When Mr. McDonald gave out a word, the student pronounced it, divided

it into syllables, told where it was accented, then gave the definition
exactly as in the speller. If the pupil missed any part of this, the teacher
gave the word out again and the speller had a second chance. If he
or she missed it a second time, the teacher made no indication, just
passed on to the next pupil and the next word. The trick was to
recognize and remember the words misspelled and when the teacher
came to you to pick up the misspelled word instead of the one he
gave out. If you correctly spelled the missed word, you passed up
the line above the pupil who missed it. The aim was to advance as
far as possible and finally to head the line. I used to hold my hands
behind me and name each finger a word in the order missed. It was
a real thrill to pick up a word no one had caught before me and
go to the head of the line!

These little triumphs were a part of the happy days when I walked
with other children to school, between times of the painful ear infec-
tions and operations that occurred frequently from 1896 to 1900. When
seeking words to describe the many times we walked the two miles
to the school on the hill, I found a passage by *Brownwood Bulletin*
columnist Joe B. Ashley, a resident of the Blanket area, who wrote
poignantly:

> We not only enjoyed school, we also enjoyed going there. We walked
> through the woods, across fields and many fences, a gate or two and dirt
> roads. There were birds to see and hear, wild plums, red haws, black
> haws, grapes, pecans and cactus apples — snow and icicles to eat, minnows
> to look for, new calves and colts to admire, running rabbits, climbing
> squirrels to chase; o'possum and skunk tracks, the soaring hawks and
> buzzards. We did not dally, however. There was lots of joking, singing,
> racing and jumping over ditches and fallen logs.

I can add that the Whiteheads' and Knudsons' two-mile walk took
us past Uncle Bunch Simpson's two big cattle tanks with just a high
dam between them to challenge us. Our mothers sternly forbade our
walking over the dam, which had deep water on each side. Carrie
and I were afraid to attempt it, but my brothers and the Knudson
boys showed off nearly every day, running and somersaulting across
the high dam and pretending to fall down the steep banks. We younger
ones were afraid to tell on the daredevils.

We did loiter as much as we dared. We picked wild flowers for our teacher, played tag, and tore off mesquite thorns with which to pull cactus "apples" from the thorny plants to eat. I didn't like the sour apples but tried to eat them, not wanting to be different. Being acutely sensitive about my impaired hearing, I avoided calling attention to any other differences from my schoolmates.

I was a towhead until I was six, when my hair began to turn blond. I wore two braids to the front of my head, both bunched into a long braid that hung down my back, tied with ribbons. All the Knudson girls had curly hair. Mrs. Knudson sat in her armless rocker with a little girl on a stool in front of her, as she dipped her comb in water and wrapped the strands around her fingers. How I longed for curls!

A little five-year-old girl in school, Ada Crozier, had black curls. We all recited little speeches at Friday afternoon "exhibitions," and I wrote some of mine. Ada was always dressed in frilly frocks and in a childish treble recited:

I am only five years old,
But I can speak a piece;
I'll tell you what we have at home—
Some chickens, ducks, and geese!

She was always applauded. I agreed she was cute—but how I hated those black curls I did not have!

I always marched proudly in the drills, especially in one where we were all birds. I was a canary. Mother could not find solid yellow goods in the Blanket store to make my canary dress; instead, she used some cloth with tiny red stars on a yellow background. Our teacher made me happy to accept this when she told me I was an exceptional bird—half canary and half redbird! I wore this dress to commencement when Professor McDonald gave me my spelling medal, and I got the first applause I ever knew. I still have a quilt that I pieced when I was nine years old that has a scrap of that dress in it.

My oldest brother, Jess, had a fine mind and at one time he showed his regret at not having more schooling. My sister Elizabeth told me how in 1893 a Blanket high-school teacher formed a special class for young people in their twenties. Jess joined the group after he and Mother worked out a schedule that they hoped he and the younger boys could keep. But they had to do the farm chores very early in the morning, walk two miles to the school, hurry home after school, pick cotton until dark, then do the feeding, milking, and other farm chores. When they got behind with the farm work, Jess had no time to study. He quit the class after two months, although he continued playing a bass drum in a school band formed during a political contest between Judge Charles Jenkins and S. W. T. Lanham for a seat in Congress.

As a very little girl, I had few contacts with Uncle Dick's family in their big white house on the hill across the railroad and the little creek from our house. His library, filled with large and, to my child's mind, unfriendly books, both scared and fascinated me. When I went with Mother to spend an afternoon with Aunt Georgia, her sister, I timidly approached the library because I loved books. Often, Uncle Dick would tell me to come in and get any book I wanted and sit on a stool near him and read. The books were beyond my reading ability, and besides, they seldom had pictures. Usually, Mother would call me away, suggesting other attractions, sometimes taking me down to the big orchard and letting me climb the trees for fruit. Uncle Dick often laughed at her. "It won't hurt her to know we are all monkeys," he would tease. This would puzzle me, although Mother tried to explain that Uncle Dick was an atheist and his big books by a man named Darwin said our ancestors were monkeys. I never understood, but I liked Uncle Dick. He loved to tell us of his experiences in the Civil War and of how he escaped capture by the Yankees many times. When my young cousin James Street was home, I enjoyed the visits. We swung across the creek on wild grapevines and coasted down a cliff in a sled made from the body of his little wagon.

Street's brothers and one sister were much older than I was but were matched up in ages with our family and were friends as well as double cousins. So when my cousin Paul, braving the opposition of an aggressive and irate neighbor, S. G. S. Thomas, ran away with Thomas's daughter Carrie, I keenly felt the excitement at our home and remember it vividly. The Thomases lived about ten miles south of Blanket. "Old Man Thomas" had a reputation as a tyrant to his family and as a suave cattleman who put on a cordial public front. It was well known that his four daughters and two sons feared his wrath and tried to maintain the subservient manner that pleased him. But when Paul, following the old-fashioned way of courting his true love, carried a ladder to Carrie's bedroom window in the dead of the night and fled with her in his speedy double-teamed buggy, the irate father, who boasted a better and faster team, followed in pursuit. But, in storybook fashion, the lovers soon reached the minister in Brownwood, as previously arranged, and were married before Mr. Thomas arrived.

The elopement was a lively topic of conversation at our house for some time, keeping me half crying with my "Why? What did they do? Why was Mr. Thomas mad?" Finally, Mother put an end to the talk and my anxiety.

"Bessie, they wanted to get married and have a home of their own. Her papa didn't want them to, but they ran away and married. That's all there is to it. Eat your dinner now."

I might add that this marriage produced four boys and four girls and a half century of apparent contentment for the parents. The youngest Thomas daughter was a close chum of mine later, and I spent many a night with her and learned to address her always polite father as "Papa," as she did. It was there that she and I ate our first persimmons, stolen slyly from a basket Papa had brought home green from somewhere and had set in the sun to ripen. This experience, causing a bitter taste and drawn, swollen lips, cemented my dislike of the fruit.

Street was Uncle Dick's youngest child. He was my brother Kirby's age, three years older than I was. When he came to our house, it was to play with Kirby, and although he was never unkind to me, as Kirby was, I was shut out of their swims in the cattle tank, their pecan hunts on the little creek, and their jaunts along the railroad track. But when Mother visited Aunt Georgia, Street played happily with me. He was always the "doctor" and I and my dolls were his patients. He concocted "medicine" for us out of bread, honey, and fruit from their big orchard and "sugar syrup" that Aunt Georgia allowed him to take from her pantries. He was a lonely child who had to play alone much of the time.

My lasting memory of Street was when his mother died. He was twelve, I was nine. Aunt Georgia had been desperately ill for several days, and Mother was with her every hour she could spare from her own family. One afternoon Street and I played on the front porch, staying near the long window of Aunt Georgia's room. He knew her condition, but he still tried to play with me. Finally, Mother came out on the porch and told him his mother wanted to see him. He went slowly inside as I watched. I felt my heart beating so fast I could hardly breathe, as I walked up and down, up and down the front steps. When Street came out he sat on the edge of the porch. I could not speak, but I stood beside him.

"Bessie, my Mama is dead," he said. "She told me good-bye and that if I will be good I'll see her in heaven. She'll be well when I see her again." He got up and walked down the porch and around the corner, dry-eyed. I fell over on the porch sobbing. Mother came out and told me a neighbor was going to take me home with her and I could spend the night with her daughter. The prospect softened my childish grief, but I dreamed that night of seeing Street walk slowly down the long porch. Street became a well-known physician in Dallas, and in our late years we kept in touch until his death in 1983.

An unexpected adventure came my way when I was about twelve, and happily it included my dear chum Carrie Knudson. Before her marriage, Mrs. Knudson was a member of the Reeves clan, one of the best-known families in Central Texas area. "Grandpa" Joseph Reeves's four sons were Matthew, Mark, Luke, and John, all married and with big families. That summer the Reeves and the Knudson families decided to take a two-week fishing and hunting trip to the Concho River pecan area some seventy miles away. Four covered wagons with mattresses, quilts and linens, and chuck boxes were prepared. Mrs. Knudson invited me to go along, and much to my surprise and joy, my mother consented.

It was two weeks of camaraderie, fun, and relaxation. There were eight adults, a few teenagers, and several small children in the group. We lounged on the big beds, played Hearts and Flinch, sang songs, and listened to the big girls tell ghost stories around the camp fires. Home-cured ham, bacon, sausage, scrambled eggs, jellies, fruits, and biscuits baked in Dutch ovens were plentiful. Even the little folks were allowed to sip the savory coffee kept hot in pots blackened by coals.

Late one afternoon, we reached a fine campsite along a little creek that ran into the Concho. While waiting for the food to cook, we kids waded in the creek and the men got out their guns to prepare for the next day's hunt. Suddenly, a horseback rider came by and the men gathered around him. He warned that a heavy rain was starting far up the river and that this campsite was often flooded.

Food was returned to chuck boxes, and everyone was hurried into the wagons. Tired and hungry, we drove to a high bank well away from the creek and river. We ate by moonlight that evening. Next day, we learned the campsite we had abandoned was under four feet of water.

For another week, the women fished and visited, the men hunted and cleaned game and fish for our camp fires, and we children played, gathered pecans, and climbed trees. By dark, we were all sleepyheads. Then misfortune again threatened.

Floyd Reeves, nine years old, was considered too young to go with the men, but was allowed to "hunt" near the camp with his BB gun. One afternoon after the men had left camp and the rest of us were in the wagons resting, Floyd set out alone to hunt birds and squirrels. He was not missed until the men returned. Concern was turning to panic when Mark, Floyd's father took his wife's hand.

"Let's not lose our heads now," he said. "We have two hours before dark. We will find him. Go ahead and prepare our meal. And pray—everybody *pray!*" The men agreed upon gunshot signals. Then each entered the woods in a different direction. The women worked quietly, and the big boys built the camp fires and cleaned fish. Margaret, Floyd's mother, nursed a smaller child and prayed in hushed tones. As the sun's rays dimmed, even the big girls crawled into the wagons, trying to stifle fear and tears.

Suddenly, Margaret called, "Floyd, Floyd, oh thank God!" We piled out of the wagons to see Floyd calmly walking into camp. Somebody grabbed a shotgun and fired two shots, and answering shots from the men came immediately. In all the hubbub, Floyd was the calmest. Mark came running into the camp and caught the boy in his arms. "Son, how did you find the way back? Did you mark your trail some way?"

"No sir. I just said, 'Jesus, I'm lost. You'll have to take me home.' And he did."

With arms lifted to the heavens, Mark led a prayer of thanks and all joined in singing.

An annual event of farm life was "hog-killing time," which came with the year's first really cold weather. This was hard, rough work for all adults. Every family raised hogs for winter meat, and neighbors helped each other to slaughter the hogs, clean them, cut the meat expertly, grind the sausage, and smoke it. Families shared the work and the meat.

I could not bear to hear the animals squeal, so I stayed in the house until the butchering ended. That was when the bladders were given to the boys to blow up for balloons. I was there then to take part, when allowed to do so. We saw real balloons only occasionally at county fairs and carnivals. At home the boys blew up the bladders, dried them, then drew straws to see who would have first chance at popping them. To do this, we put the balloon on a rock, or hard ground, put a plank over it, and then jumped on the plank. Ben or Charles would hold me to let me try.

Most of the work had to be done in bitterly cold weather. The women cut, washed, cleaned, and wrapped the smaller pieces; ground the sausage and seasoned it with salt, pepper, and sage; and then stuffed it into stocking-like cheese cloth bags made in advance. Women also dressed the hearts, livers, and sweetbreads and wrapped them for family servings. They prepared the backbones for boiling, ribs for baking, and the feet for making souse. They pared off the fat and later rendered it into lard. And what was souse? Pork trimmings finely chopped, pickled and molded into jelly loaves, considered a delicacy. Nothing was wasted on pioneer farms.

Many times, backbones and other cuts were put on to cook early, and when the work was done everybody enjoyed a feast and a visiting time. Plenty of good, hot coffee was always on the stove. It was a happy end to a hard job.

The Whitehead smokehouse was built beside our kitchen and had one outside door that was padlocked. It was our treasure house, not only for the smoked hams and bacon and meat packed in salt but also for staples bought by the barrel in Comanche or Brownwood after the harvests were sold. We younger family members were not allowed in the smokehouse, and it was impressed on us that the open door or the loss of the key were "crimes" of a momentous nature.

4.

Growing Pains and Joys

Although my childhood days were filled with love and security and simple pleasures, from six months through thirteen years, I was never really free from pain. When measles hit in the big families of that time, the very contagious disease, usually considered innocuous, attacked most members. Measles struck four of my brothers, myself, and our mother in overlapping weeks. Neighbors and other family members were the only help in such situations. My mother had the most severe case, and one of my brothers was dangerously ill. Aunt Georgia came and stayed as often as she could, and other neighbors did the same. All the heavy farm work fell on Jess, while the housework as well as nursing kept Elizabeth busy night and day. My sister Beatrice, now married, came from her farm home and stayed days at a time. Even so, in the panic of those days, I took a severe cold along with a severe form of the measles, and at one point, was given up as lost. I recovered, but the crippling aftereffects settled in my ears. Through the next several years, earaches, headaches, and dull discomfort plagued me. I learned to put this in the background and to bear it, except at times when acute attacks brought me to the big feather bed in our "fireplace room" to have warm oil, hot poultices, and other treatments prescribed by our kindly Dr. Cobb or Dr. Turney bring some comfort.

The infection grew worse. When an ear specialist in Fort Worth opened an office two days a week in Comanche, my family was grasping at straws. We had a buggy but no buggy horse, only farm work horses. As always, Elizabeth put me first. She traded her beloved mare, Moonbeam, for a buggy horse, used her school money on expenses for me and drove me to Comanche for treatments. I was then ten years old.

The treatment over several months brought no improvement. Running boils broke out behind my left ear, and drainage from them soaked my pillows. The flesh on my neck and shoulder darkened, and I lay in a coma much of the time. In despair, my family was giving me up as beyond help.

Dr. J. A. Abney, a retired physician who was a partner of my brother Jess in a small cattle investment, was asked to see me. He took one look, then told Jess to get me to Brownwood, to Dr. W. B. Anderson, the ear specialist, or, he predicted, I'd be dead in twelve more hours.

With Jess driving our hack and my other brothers holding my cot off the jolting floor, I was taken to the Brownwood train. Jess, Mother, and Sister rode in the baggage car with me, bracing my cot with baggage to hold it from careening around the floor. There was no hospital in Brownwood, so after the fifteen-mile ride I was taken to the home of Mrs. Pinckney Scott, a family friend and also a practical nurse who cared for patients in her home. There, Dr. Abney and Dr. Anderson awaited us, with a consultant, Dr. N. L. Allison. It was 6:00 P.M. on December 1, 1900.

After a brief examination, Dr. Anderson bundled up his instruments and gave them to Mrs. Scott to drop in boiling water on her cookstove. They lifted me to the big dining table that had been covered with a sheet. After Dr. Abney cut my hair, shaved my head, and administered the chloroform anesthetic, the doctors began the intricate mastoid operation. Hubert Scott, fourteen years old, and Jess held two lighted kerosene lamps as near my head as possible. The surgeons peeled away the skin, pulled out the decayed flesh, and cut away much of the big "honeycomb" bone. But after nearly an hour Dr. Anderson turned to my brother.

"If we continue, she will die on the table." Jess was drained and almost fainting. "Stop!" he said, trembling as he put his lamp down.

"You can't just let her die!" Hubert protested. When he looked again at the silent doctors, he turned away sobbing.

All that night Mother and Elizabeth sat by my cot and held cold, wet cloths to my parched lips as I begged for water that could not be given me. Dr. Anderson, who stayed until after midnight forbade water because of the danger of nausea. At 6:00 o'clock the next morning, Dr. Anderson was back.

"I am amazed," he told Mother. "She's a fighter, isn't she? It looks like she's going to live. But Mrs. Whitehead, I have to warn you that if she does, another operation will be necessary later. We had to leave decayed bone in there that will eventually have to come out."

I won that fight. As I think of it ninety years later, cameo impressions of those twenty-four hours come to me:

On our way to the Blanket station, a little boy by the roadside skittered a flat rock between the top of the carriage and my cot. My hot-headed brother Larkin dropped the leg of the cot and jumped off to chase him while the others brothers yelled at him to come back. I noticed the noise around me and tried to get off the cot.

At the station, a little girl was eating an apple, and I asked for some. Her mother cut off a piece for me, but I could not swallow it.

In Brownwood, a cart drawn by a horse carried us to the Scotts' home. I remembered the horse was a sorrel.

When my cot was carried through the hall to the dining room, I noticed the hall wallpaper had big red roses in the design. I was conscious only on and off during these hours, so I thought it a good joke when several days later I told mother about the red roses on the wallpaper in the hall. More vivid than any other memory was that of my terrible craving for water.

I lived with the Scott family for four months while I recovered from the operation. At age ten I fitted in with Belle, who was seven, and Finis, nine. My head was completely covered with a bandage that was like a white cap. Every day Dr. Anderson would come by and change the bandage. On certain days, he would scrape the "granules" in the deep hole behind my ear, causing almost unbearable pain. I would notice what instruments he wrapped in the towel that he would have Aunt Kate disinfect in boiling water. When I saw the "scraper" go in, I knew what was coming. Dr. Anderson never tried to keep me from seeing the instrument. His eyes showed his sympathy as I clenched my hands and tried not to cry. It was pain enough when the sticking gauze was pulled from the wound each day and fresh gauze packed in, but this was nothing compared to the scraping.

Living each day with playmates was a new experience. My head often suffered bumps, but I took them in my stride. I knew I was going to pay for running after the bakery wagon, when we jostled each other and often fell, but I ran anyway. The driver threw cookies and bread rolls and sometimes doughnuts into the crowd and laughed as we scrambled for the goodies. In our eighties, Finis and I through our children had a few happy years of friendship again. We once drove the Pacific coastal highway from Seattle to Los Angeles. It was a beautiful trip enlivened by small adventures.

Hubert Scott, who had held one of the lanterns during my operation, was above playing with kids. Shortly after that time, he got a job on the Santa Fe as a "butch," selling candy and magazines on the run between Brownwood and Temple. We saw very little of him. Mrs. Scott was a second mother to me. I called her "Aunt Kate," an endearment I called her all her life.

When I was well enough to return home and start back to school, I had to take a lot of teasing about my short hair. But one consolation was that the color now was a honey blond instead of a towhead white. I was twelve and had reached the shy claim-a-boyfriend stage. Friendly, outgoing Albert was my Prince Charming, and we began the taboo practice of passing notes to each other. But our romance suffered a blow when our teacher intercepted a note Albert was trying to pass to me. He had not only asked me to answer but also wrote "Harvey said ask Alice to answer his note." Caught! All four in one fell swoop. We knew what to expect. The principal paddled the boys, and Miss Bailey switched Alice's and my legs. I knew what to expect at home, too. Mother always told us if we got a whipping at school, we'd get a harder one when we got home. I did.

Next morning Albert managed to whisper sympathy and added: "Be at the side door at recess; I have something for you." I met him at recess after all the students were on the school yard. He pulled me behind the big door and daringly kissed my cheek. I can still feel his burning lips! The worst punishment to us for passing notes was that our seats were moved so that there was no opportunity to pass any more notes or even to see each other during class.

The summer of 1902 back in Blanket passed quietly, and when school opened in late September after the harvests were in I was old enough and well enough to walk the two miles there and back with neighbor children. But a small boil reappeared behind my left ear and the soreness spread again. Boils were common in those days and usually were controlled with home remedies. But this one grew larger and the pain grew also. So we made a second trip to see Dr. Anderson. Mother could not hide her worry, and I shared it.

"This is it, Mrs. Whitehead," Dr. Anderson said after a brief examination. "You remember I told you we would some day have to go after that decayed bone."

"Another operation." It was a statement, not a question, by my stoic mother. "Will she live?"

"Of course—we have every reason to think so. It will be a serious operation, but Bessie is a healthy little girl this time. She can stand it."

So it was arranged with Aunt Kate. A date was set. Dr. Abney was alerted to give the anesthetic. I was not too concerned until I realized my pretty hair, long enough for braids now, would have to come off and my head be shaved again. I complained bitterly. Dr. Abney reassured me.

"Now Bessie, you know you always wanted black hair. This time it will come back *black and curly.*"

I knew that was not so, but I loved Dr. Abney and laughed with him. Imagine my delight a few months later when it really did grow back curly!

This second operation on the same ear meant the removal of the stirrup, hammer, and anvil bones. I lived with Aunt Kate three months that time, and although the changing of the wound's dressings was as excruciating as before, I gained strength quickly and was able to hold my own with Finis and Belle and other playmates. Hubert, now sixteen, was seldom home, but when he was it was to endure a siege of asthma. He sat on the porch day and night and was so cross with us we seldom went near him. His lowering black eyes scared me, and yet he had a mysterious charm. I pictured him as a prince, and in my fantasies he would rescue me, a hopeful Cinderella. Aunt Kate, of course, cared for and protected him. Being an asthma victim herself, she understood his suffering and ill temper.

Dr. Anderson's skill and success with these two operations that were not routinely practiced at that time brought him recognition from national medical journals, and I was called a "miracle child." I had survived two major operations and a serious affliction for twelve years. But my hearing was lost completely in one ear and impaired in the other.

A last remembrance of this dear, quiet man dates from 1942 when my son, home on leave from the Navy, went with me to see him. It had been forty years since I had been his patient, possibly thirty-eight since he had seen me.

"Do you know me, Dr. Anderson?" I asked. He slowly rose from his chair and looked at me over his bifocals.

"Let me see behind your ear," he smiled.

On that visit I also saw Dr. Abney, who said, "Bessie, I stand on the bank of the river and I can see across. It looks like mighty good country to me." He died two years later at one hundred.

In 1903 we left the farm and moved to Blanket. Jess had married Emily Dudley of Zephyr, a nearby town, and they leased our home farm. My brother Larkin had married also. Kirby, the youngest, joined a professional baseball team and would leave Texas, not to return for fifty years. Charles would die suddenly of a kidney infection the next fall, the same night Jess and Emily's first son would be born. Elizabeth would teach school and attend Baylor University in alternate years until 1904, when she married a young minister. Beatrice's husband, Atison Gray, had died at thirty-two of pneumonia. Ben, who had studied pharmacy, married a Blanket girl and moved to Dublin, Texas, where he lived more than fifty years. Mother and I lived alone. I was growing up, finding every year more boring, longing for a better future, but not daring to hope for much. I wanted desperately to go to college.

Frustrated at having no further school opportunities at Blanket, I persuaded Mother to let me stay with Aunt Kate Scott in Brownwood and go to high school there. It was January, the beginning of the second semester. I was far ahead of my grade in English, but I had difficulty with math and also Latin, which was required in those days. I was discouraged but trying hard to cope when my pragmatic English teacher delivered a final blow to my hopes.

The assignment was to hand in an original short story. I was delighted. I had dozens of stories stashed away in a shoebox, so I selected one of my best love stories and turned it in. At least I'd make one A!

In class the next day I was surprised and fearful when Miss Bragg said, "Bess Whitehead, come to my desk, please." I felt curious eyes following me, the "new" girl from the country.

"I asked for an *original* story," she said, handing my paper to me. "But this *is* original," I protested, choking with embarrassment.

"This is a story copied from a love story magazine," said Miss Bragg, her wide blue eyes slaying me with scorn. With burning cheeks, I returned to my desk and picked up my books and papers. Without speaking to anyone or bothering to check out at the office, I ran all the way back to Aunt Kate's and cried my heart out in anger and despair. I refused to return to school, and when Mother came to visit at the weekend, bringing fresh vegetables and fruit from our farm, I went back to Blanket and boredom. Although the future seemed dim, I felt in my heart that some day I would join that bright world that was out yonder somewhere.

When I returned to Blanket with nothing to look forward to, I started dating a young man whose rubber-tired buggy and beautiful horse were his greatest attraction. In his early twenties, Will had a reputation as a "wild scamp." My mother objected, to no avail. Reticent Jess, in an unusual role for him, tried to warn me of Will's loose morals.

"Will and other men take women down to the Section House at night," he said. In my sheltered ignorance, my surprised reaction was "Why?" Jess gave up.

This little romance ended one night when Will showed up "in his cups." Mother told him off. I was afraid of him. He did not return, no doubt seeking more sophisticated companions. This same ignorance seemed to end my childhood romance with Albert. His family had moved to Brownwood, but Albert often came back to Blanket on weekends to be with his friends. One night as we talked in our porch swing, he asked me, point blank, "Are you going the limit with Will Jones?" Unfamiliar with the term and thinking he meant necking, a practice that was becoming a new challenge to teen-agers, I hesitantly said "yes." It was much later that I understood why Albert never came back.

Then the miracle happened.

My brother Larkin and his bride had bought homesteading land in faraway Gaines County. They were going there in their new covered wagon, driving the two work horses Larkin owned. It was June, a lax time for farm work, so Jess decided to take his wagon and team and his little family on the trek and help Larkin build a temporary house on his land. Beatrice and I went along. It was for me eight good weeks of horseback riding in the open country, helping as I could with completing the home for Larkin and Sally. In August, we started back, camping in wagon yards, eating from our chuck wagon and stopping occasionally at a hotel, where everyone enjoyed a hot bath. It was at such a stop in Midland while Beatrice and I waited in the lobby for Jess and his family to take their baths that I found the brochure on a table. The big headline jumped out at me: YOU CAN GO TO COLLEGE!

Eagerly I read about the Cottage Home System at Baylor Female College in Belton, where a girl could go a year for $108 by working two hours each day for room and board. My heart pounded as I ran across the lobby to show the astonishing announcement to Beatrice, who then worked as a practical nurse.

"Sister! [my name for her always], Look at this! Do you think we could raise $108?"

Beatrice, who all her life would give her last dime to help any of us, was as excited as I was. "I can't pay that all at once, but I can pay it out by the month."

We scanned the folder again. "Payable in advance," it read. Classes were to begin in three weeks.

"We can't make it, can we?" My disappointment was hers also, but she tried to reassure me.

"Let's not give up. Wait until Jess comes downstairs. Maybe he can find a way."

Jess had always found a way. From the time he assumed the family responsibility with my mother after our father died, he had found ways to cope. I met him at the foot of the stairs.

"Look, Jess, for just $108 I could go to college for a whole year, a whole year, but. . . ."

"But what?"

"It has to be paid in advance." Silence, as my heart raced. Jess cleared his throat.

"Well, I'll tell you," he said slowly. "I have a pair of mules I don't really need. If I can sell those mules, you can have the money."

I often told my grandchildren that Jess sent me to college on a pair of mules.

5.

College and Cottage Home in Belton

My four years in college, three at Baylor Female College in Belton (later to be the University of Mary Hardin-Baylor) and one year at Baylor University in Waco, were four of the happiest of my life. I look back as through a kaleidoscope at how Sister and I took the train from Midland back to Brownwood, where she bought goods and made her machine fly to sew me a linen suit, a dress, petticoats, underpants, and camisoles to meet the opening date at Baylor College in 1908.

My excitement about going to college grew every day, and when I finally took the train to Belton, Sister said, "Wind down now, and write us as soon as you can." Jess saw that I had a window seat. He patted my shoulder, a rare show of affection for him. "So long," was his good-bye. Sister said that as they drove back to the ranch she remarked that I'd be pretty homesick for a while, and Jess answered, "Well, Bess is always too much or too none, but she'll be all right when she gets her feet on the ground."

I did settle down a little as I started my first *real* train ride, and when a girl soon got on and took the seat beside me, I was curious enough to ask her if she was going to Belton. She said she was going to Baylor Female College, too, so we found a mutual interest. But when our train finally stopped and stood on a siding for a long time, I grew apprehensive and wondered if I was on the wrong train. We were both too embarrassed to mention our worry. When the train started backing slowly for what seemed an endless time, I was thoroughly alarmed and was greatly relieved when we finally stopped at the clearly marked Baylor station.

I had been a little apprehensive about the work I would be required to do at the Cottage Home. I need not have worried. Under the mothering hand of Mrs. Elli Moore Townsend and the firm schedules laid down by "Miss Clemmie," an older student we freshmen

Elli Moore Townsend and Lila Danforth, Baylor Female College, Belton, Texas, 1911

considered ancient, our duties were specific and changed each week. I was one of the crew that scrambled breakfast eggs this week; one of those who made coffee or filled the milk glasses next week; or helped sweep the parlors and halls the third week. Miss Clemmie saw to it that we did our work well, but also that we were never late to classes, had ample time for gym or recreation, and were in our rooms for the two-hour study hall each evening. The neglect of duties in any manner meant banishment to one's room to endure in silence a disgrace far more eloquent than a reprimand.

Not even a new girl at the Cottage Home was long in realizing that Elli Townsend was the center and moving spirit of the Home.

She greeted each one of us with love and made us know we were an important part of her "family." All during the hours we were working or busy with duties or recreation, she was among us, her black eyes caressing us, her firm voice encouraging us. She set aside thirty minutes after dinner each evening to meet with us and discuss our impressions of our new home, our needs and opinions, giving us an opportunity to air our problems. At the beginning of the year, she asked every new girl to write her a personal letter telling why she wanted to go to college, telling about her home and family, and especially telling what she wanted to make of her life. She asked us to name one seemingly impossible thing we wanted to do. I remember I told her of my great ambition to go to Europe and other countries to see and talk to people who had customs, activities, and even ideals different from ours. At our next meeting, she asked me to share my letter with the other girls and said, "I can see that Bess has a goal, and I prophesy that she will make these trips by her own efforts. To justify God's gift of life to us, we must set goals and work to attain them."

From her graduation from Baylor at Independence in 1879, Elli Townsend's goal was to help girls of ambition and limited funds to get an education. She became a faculty member at Baylor Female College in 1886, and as a special project she built a cottage that would provide an affordable home for a handful of girls. In the 1890s she resigned from teaching and for the rest of her long life raised funds to enlarge her homes and provide scholarships. Over the years, she claimed literally thousands of girls as her family. The permanent, three-story Elli-Pepper Hall was opened in 1906 with two hundred girls. I joined this group in September of 1908. Elli Moore had married Dr. E. G. Townsend in 1899, and in 1915 they transferred the entire Cottage Home system and property to the Texas Baptist State Convention. The hundreds of girls that still enjoy the benefits of this self-help institution must be judged by the standards of "self-control, self-sacrifice, and purity of mind" set by this deeply religious and deeply caring woman, who died in her home on the campus of what is now Mary Hardin-Baylor University.

I've never aspired to being a poet, but since early childhood, I have found pleasure in writing verses in appreciation of friends I have

admired. I was inspired by Mrs. Townsend to set goals for my life
and strive to reach them. She was a beloved model. I told her so
in verse and sent it to her by a student friend.

To Elli M. Townsend

It seems to me the very light that shone
    From countenance of Christ in days of old
    Is mirrored in your eyes. In perfect mold
His life by love is blended with your own.
Like Him you've walked Gethsemane alone
    And borne the cross that others might behold
    The gifts of God. And in your heart is sown
The seeds of peace that naught but wisdom hold.
Oh friend, to us whose faith has not been tried,
    Who need the clasp of hand—a word, a sign,
    You are a tower of strength, a beacon guide,
A living well of truth and love divine.
It seems to me that always by your side
The lights of God in benediction shine.

Mrs. Townsend came by the cottage where Mother and I lived
and thanked me. She was deeply moved. She told Mother I was a
"talent blessed by God." She predicted I would reach any worthy
goal I set and would always be a blessing to Baylor. Mother welcomed the visit and the tribute. I was pleased but somewhat embarrassed. Mrs. Townsend donated her last several years to raising
money for her goal—making it possible for girls without funds to
work their way through Baylor College. She had the verse I wrote
printed in script on attractive cards and used it in her campaigns.
Years after I gave it to her, when she had organized several student
leagues to help raise funds for scholarships, Mrs. Townsend wrote
me that largely due to the tribute I wrote she had that month received a donation of five thousand dollars to the cottage home. She
wrote:

We were inspired at Judd Mortimer Lewis' election for Poet Laureate
of Texas to elect a Poet Laureate for the Student League. . . . It was voted
that you, as an ex-student . . . should be our first Student League Poet
Laureate. So many nice things are being said about your poem. . . . I

read your verse and strive to attain those qualities. I feel very humble. I cannot express in words how much I value your friendship. You must give yourself over to writing. You have a rare gift.

Saturday night was fun night at the Cottage Home, given to visiting, games, music sessions, or plays, adapted or original, with the Thespians vying with one another in making original costumes. Of course, in this all-female college we had to take the male parts, and this was the only time we were ever allowed to wear pants. Shorts were taboo, even in our plays, and for our basketball, tennis, and gym, all of which I loved, we wore black bloomers, long black stockings, and middy blouses. On Sundays, we marched in pairs the quarter mile to the First Baptist Church, wearing uniforms of navy blue suits, white blouses, and high-topped black shoes. The uniform and church attendance were required of the Luther Hall "rich girls" too.

As to boyfriends—we had none. Only a brother or a cousin could ever visit us briefly in the dormitory parlors, and seldom did a phony "cousin" make the grade. In the three years I was at Baylor Female College, only one girl was expelled, and it was because a "cousin" helped her out of a dormitory window to spend an evening in town. She was a petite, popular senior. A pall lay over the campus the day she was expelled. A funeral could not have been more depressing.

Although I had enjoyed many boyfriends before I went to Baylor, handsome, outgoing Albert being a favorite, I did not miss them at Baylor. I was too busy. Happy in making new friends, working, and vying with classmates to make the highest grades filled my days. I loved the athletics and was very competitive. I made my B in basketball, was a forward on the six-member first team, and was an avid tennis player. Our coach was George Rosborough, a Belton native who was accepted on campus almost as another teacher. I think he enjoyed pitting his players against each other; he certainly enjoyed seeing each of us reach the top. In my senior year, 1911, a junior girl and I split the honors in tennis and the spring Field Day events— races, hurdles, jumps, javelin, throws, all of it.

Although I had met Lila Danforth, who was to be my dearest friend, early in this first year at Baylor, she did not share these activities with me. She was not athletically inclined; also, her time out

The author at Baylor Female College, Belton, Texas, 1911

of classes was devoted to her invalid mother, who died in our senior year. But, she was my greatest fan and shared in my triumphs.

I adored my teachers and worked as hard for their approval as I did for my own benefit. Mathematics was always my waterloo. Science was also a hard subject for me. But I loved Dr. E. H. Wells, a dear old man who taught these subjects and quietly demanded that his students give every ounce of their abilities to learning them. Through plane and solid geometry, algebra, and physics and chemistry, I tried (and often cried) and with Mr. Wells's help made B's and C's, seldom an A. But in Shakespeare classes, history, and Latin and Greek, I excelled.

Martha Dowell, who taught Latin, after the first four weeks of school became my mentor, my savior, the shining star of my aspirations. She reached my heart and soul and made me her slave for life through her sensitive understanding of my physical handicap that I always tried so desperately to hide.

When I entered Baylor College from the unaccredited high school of Blanket, I had to take four subjects but qualified for only two, English and history. The college offered the Bachelor of Literature, the Bachelor of Science, and the classic Bachelor of Arts degrees. In my first week, I had heard the girls speak in such scorn of the B.L. ("Be Lazy") degree that I knew I did not want that. I also doubted I'd ever make the B.S. (science and math). So I had to sign up for the B.A. Classic—majoring in Greek and Latin. I had already had an unfortunate bout with high-school Latin, attempting to enter a class at mid-term and failing to catch up with the first-year grammar. So I feared Latin and rebelled at having to take it. But I could not break the college requirements. Miss Dowell assigned me to her class. She was a tall, large-framed woman with long ash-blond hair that she wore piled on top of her head. Her profile was decidedly stern; she looked like Juno. I felt I was in for a rough year.

On the first day of class, I made for the back row of seats, persuading Lila to go along with me. Progress in the first two weeks did not change my dislike for the subject. Then, on Friday of that second week, Miss Dowell asked me to stay after class for a few minutes. I felt I had failed before I started and walked up to her desk, my knees trembling.

"Bess," she said, "you are hard of hearing, aren't you?"

I was too astonished to answer at once. She continued.

"I know you feel embarrassed about it, feeling you are different. But you'd be surprised, my dear, to know how many of us do not hear perfectly. I do not, and neither does Dr. Wilson." He was the college president.

"But I have a greater handicap," she continued. "I have to wear bifocal glasses, see?" She raised her head and peered down at me comically. "And I can't even see to read unless I have the glasses on."

She had me smiling.

"Now, I wish you and Lila would sit on this second row in front of me so I can *see you* better and you can *hear me* better. Will you do that?"

She talked to me another ten minutes, telling me she could see that I was a serious student and that I could do anything I wanted to in life if I would accept my "little handicap" and work around it.

She took me to the door, her arm around my shoulder. For the next three years, I worked to learn Latin and Greek as I had never worked before. I translated the Latin poems in verse form and wrote original plays in Greek, using the Greek characters we studied. Miss Dowell was delighted. I corresponded with her long after I left Baylor. She wrote to me of her marriage and her new home in Tennessee. I wrote to her of my children. When I heard she had died suddenly, my tears fell on the dress I was ironing for my little girl as I composed a poetic tribute to my great and lovely friend.

After one year in the Cottage Home in Belton, my mother and I moved into one of the Townsend Apartments at the edge of the college campus, in the same house with my friend Lila and her parents. In our junior year, Baylor Female College became an oddity—a three-year college. The curriculum was raised one year. This caused the thirty-plus candidates for graduation in 1911 to reassess their credits. Only nine of us qualified as seniors in September of 1910. I was among these because my brother Jess again came to the rescue. He paid for a four-week session of summer school in Baylor University for me to make the two additional credits I needed. Lila was also among the nine seniors.

We had a memorable year. We named ourselves the nine Muses, and our parties and class projects followed the theme. I was Euterpe, Goddess of Lyric Poetry, and was elected class poet. We did not have a school newspaper, but we filled our yearbook with verses, essays, plays, and giddy cartoons. We really were faculty "pets," and because our group was small, we were allowed to go to special events in town—well chaperoned, of course. Every one of us won individual honors in our fields, and when it came time to award the annual scholarship for Baylor University, no less than five of our nine qualified as to character and grades. It was given to me because of a third criterion—need.

Each graduate in those days read an original graduation essay. I

The author at the time of her graduation from Baylor Female College, Belton, Texas, 1911

had made my mark for three years by writing and by special excellence in Latin and Greek. So, looking back, I am puzzled at the subject I chose for my commencement essay. I read from the high stage podium, surrounded by a mass of sweet peas that almost choked by their permeating fragrance, my interpretation of "Alfred Tennyson and His Four-Dionysian Poem: In Memoriam."

In June of 1911, I returned to Jess's ranch near Brownwood, where I spent most of the summer. I asked him and my brother Ben, a businessman in nearby Dublin, if they would lend me the money for my 1911–1912 year in Baylor University. I had received the tuition scholarship, but I did not have the opportunity to work for my room and board there. They agreed, and I assured them that although my goal was to become a newspaper reporter and writer I would first take a teaching job to pay off that debt. There was an understood verity in our family: your just debt was paid *first*, then your money was yours. We signed no contract. Our word was our bond.

6.

Fun and Romance at Baylor University

A new world opened for me when I settled into Georgia Burleson Hall at Baylor University in Waco, Texas, during September, 1911. Not the least of this world were boys. Only the buildings in the rectangle now called Old Baylor made up the school then: Old Main, the Library, the Science Hall, Burleson and Brook dormitories, and the Academy, where freshmen who lacked certain high-school credits could make up those courses. All the classes met in the Library Building and the Science Hall. The parlors, dining hall, and kitchens were in Old Main. My courses were advanced Latin and Greek, biology, philosophy, analytical geometry, and creative writing; this last course was an elective offered for the first time in Baylor and was taught by Professor Dorothy Scarborough, who later became a nationally known writer. This was the icing on my cake. "Miss Dottie" sponsored the *Baylor Literary,* a monthly magazine primarily for printing the work of her class. We were a prolific group of writers, some of us having one to three creations in each issue.

> Yet ah, that spring should vanish with the rose!
> That youth's sweet-scented manuscript should close.

Thus Zenus Black, a classmate, opened a series of articles that he called "The Baylor Sketch Book." Today, after eighty years, these lines bring to my heart the same mysterious sadness and romance as then, although mellowed by experience and a better understanding of the sweet spring of youth. Zenus was older than most of us in the class, a loner who rarely took part in discussions and resisted Miss Dottie's efforts to draw him out. We recognized him as an exceptional writer. He was a handsome man, and we girls wanted to flirt with him but didn't dare. Watching him walk by me one day, seemingly unaware of my existence, inspired the verse that later won first place in the 1912 Annual Intercollegiate Press Association contest.

WELL, MAYBE SO

They say the birds sing jes' as sweet
And jes' as cheery, too,
As any other day they did—
And skies is jes' as blue.
Well, maybe so. I do not know
Jes' what the matter be;
I only know on yesterday
You didn't smile at me.

They say the world rolls on the same
And grass is jes' as green,
And every dawn the sunrise brings
Is brightest ever seen.
Well, maybe so. But I jes' know
The sunshine I can't see.
It's awful dark since yesterday,
You didn't smile at me.

It was sheer joy to see my verses, stories, and bylines in print each month. It was a highlight of my year when Miss Scarborough called me to the stage in April of 1912 to pin on my red sweater two gold medals given by the IPA for best short story and best poem.

Those were the days of daily chapel in the second floor of the library building; of Lynn Wood at the pipe organ; of Margaret Terry (later Harrell), the patient and sympathetic "Miss Margaret," monitor of the second floor of Burleson Hall sacred to seniors; of Prexy Brooks and his stories of the boys from "Pull Tight" and "Hog Wallow"; of Dean Kesler and his biology bugs; of Professor Phelan and his "little boy Kenneth"; of Big Henry, football hero, and Coach Ralph Glaze; of Hoggie Bunkley, tennis star; Odie Minatra, the editor; Hal Lattimore, the orator; Tommy Dowell, class comedian; Autie Marrs, chatterbox, et cetera; the days of the Turkey Trot at Brooks Hall and of the meningitis epidemic when the password was "Bow your head and spray"—dear, sweet-scented manuscript of youth! A year in Baylor, a lifetime of treasured memories! A year with interesting people who helped mold my life.

When I was a student there in 1911–12, rebellion was spelled with a lower case "r." Only a daring attempt at hazing by kidnapping that fall caused even a ripple on campus. But, twenty-five years later during President Pat Neff's administration in 1938, a "yellow sheet" calling Neff a Nazi, Der Führer, Il Duce, and Emperor Hirohito, was circulated. The charge against Neff: censorship of "free speech." The administration was criticized for its stand against students "shooting off their mouths" and writing articles for the student newspaper expressing the opinions that students were losing "all power of independent judgment" and becoming "mere unthinking collectivists." The sheet was titled "Il Poplo," and there were swastikas drawn on the masthead. The tirades were answering President Neff's ultimatum against criticism that seemed rampant on campus, in the *Lariat* (the campus newspaper), and in cafes. Neff read some of the yellow-sheet comments to the student body in morning chapel and requested a vote on the statements. Although some fifty students approved, the majority disapproved and some one hundred chose not to vote. Result: Carey Williams, Raymond Smith, and Elton Miles, editors of the "Sheet," were indefinitely suspended from Baylor. Williams was refused permission to speak on the subject in chapel, and campus groups discussing the situation were dispersed, with threat of suspension. Although I was in Houston by this time, working on the *Houston Post,* a young student friend at Baylor wrote to me at length, thinking I might air the affair in the *Post.* He wrote, "You can't imagine the feeling on the campus. It is a most uncomfortable situation. Everybody here is nervous."

Yes, I could imagine the resentment, the fear, and the sadness felt on that quiet campus so many years ago. I compare in my mind the frequent student rebellions of today, some that even result in lawsuits against schools, charging suppression of freedom of speech.

As I look back once again, some of my more vivid memories of interesting people relate to persons I knew at Baylor University, especially two whose friendship and guidance helped shape my life: "Miss Dottie" Scarborough, teacher of creative writing, and Dr. Samuel Brooks, president of Baylor and a father-friend to all students.

I see Miss Dottie, slender and youthful, enthusiastic, fragile in appearance but really a robust sprite who skipped along the walk from the Science Building to Old Main, with swirling skirts. She always seemed as young as we, her pupils, who were in our early twenties, but in talents and experience her real age was mid-thirties. We adored her and basked in her pride in us and her untiring zeal to encourage our amateur efforts at publication in our monthly magazine the *Literary*. I consider myself exceptionally blessed to have been in her class. Miss Dottie is given credit for founding the first college department of journalism in the Southwest.

Dorothy Scarborough taught several years at Baylor, then at Columbia University, where she earned her doctorate. She wrote five novels, including the controversial *The Wind,* which was made into a movie starring Lillian Gish, who at that stage in her life really resembled Miss Dottie. *The Wind* was reprinted in the 1980s and again became a popular presentation of West Texas and the tragic effects of wind and isolation on the characters in the story. She also wrote about folklore and folk songs that today are valuable reference material.

My heart always thrills as I look back over nearly a century to see Miss Dottie, and I am reminded of Shelley's lines, so appropriate to her, "an angel still," inspiring and unforgettable—"a lovely lady, garmented in light from her own beauty."

It was also my good fortune to be in Baylor when the indomitable Prexy Brooks was the president of the University. We all knew that Dr. Brooks's foremost concern was for the students. He laughed with us and wept with us, his Baylor children. He was noted for his integrity, his moral and physical courage. Several years later, when Baylor alumni learned that on his deathbed he had managed to sign well over three hundred of the many diplomas awarded that year, we were filled with admiration but not surprise. "Just like Prexy," we said.

In the first month of this happy year, the president of the senior class asked me, a new girl, to be his date at the first senior social affair. This did not make me a favorite of the other senior girls, most of whom were in their fourth year. But it made me solid with the boys. I never lacked for dates.

I enjoyed this unexpected popularity, but in retrospect I can see that some of this might have been because my naiveté challenged the senior men to test that innocence. Sheltered at home and guarded in a girls' school where even "cousins" were persona non grata, my attitude was real but invited testing. At the first soirée of the year, an attentive escort slowly led me through laughing groups until we were partially hidden by a stairway. He put his arm around my shoulder and lightly touched my breasts, calling them "twin sanctuaries." I could not look at him. "Forgive me, I love you," he whispered. I fled to my room. I dared tell only my roommate, sworn to secrecy. We whispered about the daring swain until long after the lights were out. I was thrilled, but dreaded seeing him the next day. I need not have worried. He evidently was convinced I was an ignorant but "nice" girl. He avoided me. In time, we became casual friends.

By Christmas, I had settled down to one "sweetheart." Hal was debonair, handsome, and one of the most popular men in Baylor. He was a football star, a member of the top debate team, and president of the Erisophian Society, one of two men's societies in the school. What more could a girl ask?

These carefree days passed swiftly. I missed the competitive sports I had enjoyed at Baylor Female College. In the university, the girls had only gym classes, and seniors were excused from these. We posed in fake tennis and basketball pictures for the yearbook. But the football games, debate contests, senior picnics, soirées in the dormitory parlors, and the big program of the year by the two women's societies and the two men's societies were outstanding events. The competition was keen, and the original programs, worked on for weeks, were kept as surprises until the nights they were presented. The women's societies were the Calliopean and the RCB Society. The men's were the Erisophian and the Philomathesian.

I was a member of the Calliopean Society. After much discussion, we decided to put on Tennyson's long poem *The Princess,* and I was asked to write it in dramatic form. With the help of Miss Margaret, I wrote the play, revising and condensing until we had a sixty-minute production of three acts, each act having two or three scenes. We assigned all of the parts and chose a very beautiful, auburn-haired junior as the Princess.

Other society members planned songs and tableaux acts for the between-act periods. We ordered white Grecian princess-style costumes from Dallas, and the members of our brother society, the Erisophian, made or procured all our props, including a white-and-gold throne for the Princess. We rehearsed faithfully until everything was letter-perfect.

The author appearing in her dramatization of Tennyson's The Princess *at Baylor University, Waco, 1912*

On Wednesday before the Friday-night program, a bomb fell. The dean's office routinely reviewed the record of our players. Students who had ten demerits, or worse, were barred from participation in public programs.

Our Princess had ten demerits.

Weeping and wailing. Woe and calamity. They wouldn't dare! But they did.

Dean Kesler was adamant. Miss Dottie, who had read and approved our script, was crushed along with us but felt she could not interfere.

Miss Margaret and I went to our adored President Brooks. He sympathized with us but told us that it would "open the flood gates" if he made an exception to the rule and that he could not do so.

Miss Margaret pulled us out of the dumps. She declared we would not be stopped; there was always a way.

"Bess wrote the play and has directed it. She knows every line as no one else does. She will play the Princess, and the show will go on!"

I had never aspired to acting. I was a writer, I protested. But she was right. I was the only one who knew all the lines. Dr. Brooks let the cast miss Thursday and Friday classes (even excusing any who had tests!) and we practiced Wednesday night, Thursday, and Thursday night. Because I was prompter, too, I had to sit on the throne with a bell beside me for signaling changes, exits, entrances, etc. Miss Margaret prompted from the wings. The show went on.

The side balconies of the auditorium overhung the stage at the ends, and as I walked under the overhang in one scene of the first act, a note fluttered down at my feet. I picked it up, and as I walked to the throne glanced at it: "You are great, honey. You are MY Princess! (Hal)."

Graduation events that spring were the climax of a wonderful year. My remembrance of them are still with me. The seniors planted a tree. I wrote "Ode to a Tree" for the occasion. I wore a new dress, white with a small blue figure the gods sent me by my sisters Elizabeth and Beatrice.

My mother was there to watch her "baby," whom she came so near losing, receive her diploma. My roommate knocked my white shoes, wet from cleaning, off our second story window onto the cinder-covered ground. In rescuing and recleaning them, I was almost late for the march to get our diplomas. I was saved by my name, which, in alphabetical order, put me at the end of the line. Later, when Hal took Mother and me to the train to go to Brownwood, he kissed my cheek and then kissed Mother. Startled, she patted his shoulder and said, "Oh pshaw!"

Most of my closest associates at Baylor have passed on, but memory of them is vivid and lasting. In past years, I have renewed friendships with a few who attended the Heritage Club organized in 1976 for alumni who attended Baylor more than fifty years ago. A program and banquet for these pioneers is sponsored by the club each spring, and each member of the class celebrating its golden anniversary is given fiftieth-anniversary diplomas. We reminisce, recalling friends and incidents of our past. Speakers arouse pride in our school, which was chartered by the Republic of Texas in 1845 and, of the nineteen institutes of higher learning chartered by the Republic, is the only one still in existence. At the 1986 gathering, graduates of 1910–11 and 1912 were honored. In 1987, the Texas Pioneer Village given to Baylor by Bill and Vada Daniel of Liberty, which is located adjacent to the expanded Strecker Museum, was visited. At the Heritage Club banquet, I was presented my Diamond Anniversary diploma.

Every year when the Baylor Heritage Club meets, I find with surprise that very few of the old-timers know how and why green and gold became Baylor's colors. Sara Rose Kendall (1902) answered that question in a letter now filed in the Texas Collection at the Baylor Library. She wrote:

I was a member of the committee that chose the colors. This is the true story:

In the year of 1897, Baylor and Add-Ran, now Texas Christian University, held a debate in Bryan, Texas. A train on the Texas Central Railroad took the Baylor crowd to Bryan. It was spring, and our train passed through a field abloom with wild dandelions. The vivid yellow and green were beautiful together and someone on the train said, "What a lovely combination." I turned to Charlie Ingram, the other member of the committee and said, "Charlie, there are our colors except that we will say 'green and gold' instead of green and yellow if you like the idea." He did, and we recommended them to the proper authorities and they were adopted, probably in 1897. The colors were first used in Lorena, Texas, at a concert given by the Baylor Glee Club on Friday, March 25, 1897.

Faculty members of the past who are among the most interesting people remembered are two that made me feel out of the ordinary. Dr. J. W. Downer, Latin professor, always greeted me with a smile and a fatherly pat on the shoulder. He often read my translations of Horace's Odes and Epodes aloud to our class, because I wrote my translations in Horace's own poetic style and rhythm. Since most of the class members were studying for the ministry, they were not too impressed. Nevertheless, the recognition fed my ego and was reassuring to a country girl still not comfortably at home in the big university.

About the same recognition was repeated in the Greek class each day. We were reading "Demosthenes on the Crown." In my previous years in Baylor Female College in Belton, I had been so thoroughly coached in Greek that I could read Demosthenes as well as I could English—which I did. Dr. Henry Trantham showed his approval in less effusive manner than Dr. Downer, but he did show it. In an offhanded manner on the first morning he remarked, "It is evident that Miss Whitehead has done her homework." The implication was not lost on my classmates, who in time accepted me as a studious, although possibly naive, newcomer.

Even with many years to think about it, I could never catalogue Dr. J. B. Johnson, my teacher of analytical geometry. He knew some kind of trick awaited him every day, and he evidently figured that the only way to spoil the joke for the perpetrators was to play back one of his own. As he walked to his desk, he took his derby from his head and threw it at a wire hook that was supposed to project from the wall by the door. We knew and he knew that the wire, which was a short length of an electric cord that had formerly been linked to the wall light, had been shoved back in its hole in the wall. So his derby bounced to floor, where a half dozen boys chased it. When they deferentially put the derby on his desk, Dr. Johnson promptly put it on his head. Various oddities frequently showed up in the room, and perhaps Dr. Johnson would take ten minutes or more to chalk in wild markings for a complicated problem on the board. He might erase the problem in the next minute, but again he might not. So we did not dare ignore it. Too often it showed up in a test question later. Sometimes the boys would stack chairs in neat ladders on the prof's desk. He would take his seat at the desk behind the chairs and, hidden, talk to us through the barricade. If we lost what he was saying and did not take notes, we regretted it on the next test day.

Hal, that happy extrovert from a pioneer Texas family of character, talent, and achievement and of comfortable economic status, I think never knew what a green isle in an enchanted sea he was to me that year. He made me feel important, wanted, and loved. By graduation, we were "tentatively" engaged, but years of separation—law school for him, teaching for me—were too much for young love. We lost touch.

7.

New Directions

I left Baylor University in June, 1912. Two years of teaching in high schools and college followed. The 1914–15 academic year in Howard Payne College in Brownwood was a stressful one. Europe went to war against Germany. Our young men joined combat services. War hysteria grew. Uncertainty and financial problems began to deplete the colleges, especially the church-supported ones. Howard Payne, a church college, was facing closure. Teachers left as paychecks were cut, then discontinued entirely. Raised in Baptist churches and graduated from Baptist colleges, I, with a few other teachers, stayed through May of 1915, when the session closed, receiving only room and board at the teachers' dormitory during the spring months.

I had contracted to teach two levels of Latin and one of Greek, assist with themes in the English department, and serve certain hours in the library. When the year closed, I was teaching four levels of Latin and two levels of Greek, helping grade themes in the English department, and holding all my classes in the library to keep it open! But I also had made the final payments on my debt to my brothers.

Looking back, I feel a certain pride that I may have helped a school grow into a fine university that now serves the Central and West Texas area. Although on the windy May day when my brother came for me and my trunk in the ranch pickup, I was feeling pretty low and quite a bit fearful of what lay ahead.

"Jess," I said as we rode to his ranch near Brownwood, "I have one dime in my purse from this year of teaching. But I have paid you and Ben back and don't owe anybody a cent. Lila has invited me to go to Houston and live with her until I get a job. I'm going down there and try to get into newspaper work."

"Well," he said laconically, "looks like you can't go anywhere but up." The next day he gave me twenty-five dollars "to get started" in Houston. I was twenty-five years old, still an unsophisticated small-town girl.

Again Sister came out to the ranch and helped me get together needed clothes for my new adventure in Houston. My friend Lila Danforth had written, inviting me to stay with her and her father while I tried to break into the newspaper field. Jess made reservations on the Santa Fe, and at 11:00 P.M. on May 20, 1915, I was on my way. Since the train would reach Houston at an early hour, I did not take a Pullman. I napped very well in my chair until a man took a seat beside me. I had been taught by family and custom not to speak to strange men. I felt him looking at me, but I avoided his eyes and picked up the book I had been reading. He was having none of that.

"Do you get off at Houston?" he asked very casually. I was taught to be polite, too.

"Yes."

"Do you live there?"

"No."

I was not a vain girl, but I knew I was an attractive, somewhat buxom blond. He was challenged. I felt his amusement at my discomfiture, and to my disgust I felt my face burning.

"Have you ever eaten the luscious immense strawberries they serve at the Harvey House in Houston?"

"No." I had rarely eaten strawberries of any size. They did not grow in Brown County.

"Well, they are something you shouldn't miss. How about eating breakfast with me at the Harvey House?"

How was I going to deal with this? Wonder if I should call the conductor. No, I can't be that silly. I'll just be firm with him. "Thank you. My friend will meet me in Houston, and we will go to her house for breakfast." I've told a lie! Lila will be at work by eight. I'm to take a cab to her house.

"Oh, I see," he said with a smile. "Then both of you eat strawberries with me at the Harvey House."

Well, that's better. Maybe he's just being friendly. "I'm sure she will have to hurry. She works."

I opened my book again and he was silent.

Now, I must get out of his sight quickly at the depot and find a cab. I hope he doesn't watch to see if Lila meets me!

But he did watch, and he saw my uncertainty as I looked for the cab stand. He took his hat off as he came toward me. "Little girl," he said seriously (I weighed 125 pounds and was twenty-five years old), "I know you don't trust me, but I'm harmless. My name is Jim Cook, and I travel for a Dallas company. I like to make friends and have someone to talk with. If your friend is not here and you want a taxi, I'll get one. But if you're not in a hurry, why not eat breakfast with me, and then I'll put you in a taxi to send you where you want to go."

He could see I was melting. "That's the ticket! This way!" He opened the door and held it for me. I'm glad to say we had a hearty breakfast, starting with the biggest, reddest strawberries I had ever seen. Mr. Cook told me about his wife and little girl in Dallas. I told him about my friend Lila and my experience in Howard Payne College. He spoke seriously about the war in Europe and predicted the United States would be sending men over in less than a year. An hour later, he thanked me for a friendly visit, put me in a taxi, paid the fare, and sent me on the way—intact.

After a weekend of renewing friendship with Lila and Dad Danforth, and with their blessing, I was ready to brave the dens of the *Houston Post* editors. A warm drizzle, typical spring weather for Houston, beaded my rain hat as I walked toward the lobby of the *Post* building at Texas and Travis streets. My hands were clenched in an effort to calm my nerves. I walked slowly to the elevator. It was May 26, 1915.

"I want to see Judd Mortimer Lewis," I told the elevator operator.

"Fourth floor," he said mechanically. I felt him watch me with mild curiosity as I hesitated before getting out at the fourth floor.

"To your left, lady. All the way to the end." I was relieved when he closed the door and started down. All the way to the end, all the way to the end my racing heart and slow footsteps echoed.

The office door was open and I stepped into the world of my dreams and into a career that would continue for more than seventy years. Smiling blue eyes looked at me from behind a cluttered desk. "Come in, young lady. I'm Judd Lewis. Were you looking for me?"

Lila Danforth and the author at the beach in Galveston, 1915

All my life I had wanted and tried to write—childhood verses, teenage romances, college essays, and "poetry," all the while confident that some day I would find a place on a big newspaper. I had never even seen a big city room, but this solid ambition had grown through school and college, through three years of teaching in small-town schools. My goal was twofold: a college degree and a newspaper career. I had won the first, now for the second. I had been repeatedly warned how difficult it would be for a woman. But now, I made the plunge.

Judd Mortimer Lewis was only a name to me, known through his column that ran for many years on the *Post*'s editorial page. His

The author with W. T. ("Dad") Danforth, Houston, 1915

was the only name on the newspaper I knew. I looked into his friendly eyes as he ran his hand over a bald pate fringed by blond curls and was encouraged.

"I don't know who to go to, but I know your name because I read your column. I want to work on the *Post*." I spoke hurriedly while my courage lasted.

Mr. Lewis smiled. "Well now, it's nice you remembered me. But you want to see Mr. Harry Warner, our managing editor. Come with

me, and I'll take you to him." I'm sure he could see how frightened
I was, and he talked continuously as we walked down the corridor
to the city room. No, I told him, I had no experience. Yes, I liked
to write. He assured me, "There is a place for all bright young people who love to write."

"Now, this is Mr. Warner's corner," he continued as he led me
past reporters' desks with battered typewriters and through aisles
strewn with crumpled-up newsprint obviously thrown on the floor
by the same busy reporters. "You see, he has just a little fence around
his corner of this big city room so he can see the boys out there
and keep tabs on everything. He's the boss.

"I see he's not here just now. It's about 2:30, so that means he's
over at Kelly's for a cup of coffee. Why don't you sit at this desk
here and read these newspapers? He'll be back soon."

I thanked Mr. Lewis, who I learned later was the Poet Laureate
of Texas, and sat in the creaking swivel chair. I had my back to the
city room and was looking eagerly at the newspapers open on the
desk, the *New York Times, Boston Transcript, St. Louis Post-Dispatch* —
what a wealth of reading! I was soon buried in them, oblivious to
people and place.

Suddenly, I realized someone was standing beside me. I looked
up, startled by a giant of a man peering down at me. His keen blue
eyes looked over glasses perched on the end of his nose, and his mouth
was hidden behind a fierce looking mustache.

I was speechless.

"Well," he drawled finally. "Is this the new managing editor?"

"Yes, sir," I blurted out defensively. "What can I do for you?"

I caught my breath at my own audacity. What had I said? I
looked down in embarrassed silence. Mr. Warner gave a dry chuckle.

"Oh," he said. "Now Miss Managing Editor, if you'll let me have
my chair and you sit over here, I'll see what I can do for *you*." I
was already out of his chair and standing by another. He motioned
me to sit, but I felt the need to anchor myself to the back of the
chair.

"I didn't mean to be rude. . . ."

He cut in. "Never mind about that. Did you want to see me?"

"Yes sir," I took myself in hand and spoke deliberately. "I want to work on the *Post*. Mr. Lewis said for me to see you."

"Lewis? Does Judd recommend you for a job?"

"Oh, no sir. I don't know Mr. Lewis. I went to him because I like his column. He sent me to you."

"Do you think you can write his column?" His sarcasm stung, but I was determined.

"Of course not. Not yet, anyway. But I want to learn the newspaper business. I *know* that's what I want to do."

He became serious. "Young lady, we do not have any vacancies on the paper. We have society and women's club editors, and Miss Willie Hutchinson is our music editor. These are the only women we need on our staff."

"But I don't want to write about those things," I explained earnestly. "I want to write news stories and stories about people, unusual things."

His eyes bored into me over his glasses. "Have you had any experience?" he asked sharply.

"No, sir. But I can do it. I want to learn. I'll work for nothing—"

"We don't use women on the city side."

"Sir?"

"The city side. That means the newsroom. We have women, but only in the women's department." His words sounded final.

I couldn't back down now. I was desperate.

"Mr. Warner," my crisp voice surprised myself. "This is mid-1915. Europe is at war, and everybody knows we will be in it within another year. Your young men will have to go to war. You'll *have* to train women for their jobs!"

He looked at me in silence.

"Sit down," he said finally.

As I sat down and drew my raincoat around me, I tried again. "I want to *learn*. I can work for nothing through the summer if you'll let me. I don't know any other way to learn. And I *can* do it."

Mr. Warner adjusted his glasses and idly stroked his mustache. "I'll tell you what I'll do," he said slowly. "I won't have anybody working for me for nothing. I'll give you six dollars a week for two weeks. If at the end of two weeks you are not worth that to me, out you go!"

"That's fair enough," I gulped.

"But you are on your own, remember. I have no assignments for you. You'll have to find your own 'people and things' to write about."

I faltered a bit but was game. "Yes, sir," I agreed.

He turned to me suddenly. "Can you use a mill?" he demanded. I'm sure I looked as nonplussed as I felt.

"A mill!" he repeated, and pointed to his typewriter. My heart fell. I shook my head.

"Now, ain't *that* something?" He showed his annoyance. "Can you write so a typesetter can read it?"

I bridled. "Yes sir, I can write a very good hand."

"All right. Here is copy paper, here is a big-leaded pencil. Here is a proof of a picture of a high-school graduating class and a letter telling the names of the students in the order in which they stand by rows, left to right. Sit at that table in the corner and write me a cutline."

A cutline? I thought I knew what he meant, and I was determined not to ask. He knew. He picked up a newspaper and silently pointed to the caption under a picture. I nodded and walked to the table.

I carefully read the information in the letter, grateful that the managing editor had turned back to his desk. In a firm, bold hand I wrote my first newspaper cutline on the proof. I laid it on Mr. Warner's desk. He ignored it but swivelled his chair and looked at me over his glasses.

"Remember, you are on your own. I'm a busy man; don't ask me any fool questions."

On that day in 1915 when I persuaded Mr. Warner to give me a chance to learn the newspaper world as a *Houston Post* cub, Houston was a city of approximately 78,000 inhabitants. Ben Campbell was mayor. James E. Ferguson was Texas governor, and William P. Hobby, later to own the *Post*, was lieutenant governor. Morris Sheppard and Charles Culberson were U.S. senators from Texas, and J. H. Davis and Jeff McLemore were Texas congressmen. Houston's post office had six substations, all under the direction of Postmaster Thomas W. House. B. B. Davidson was police chief.

Houston Heights, with James B. Mannion as mayor, was a separate city, as was Magnolia, with Mayor William McKenzie. There were more than 156 churches of many denominations. Fred W. Horn was superintendent of Houston's public schools, and Rufus Cage was president of the school board. Sam Houston was the only high school for white students, and Booker T. Washington served as a junior and senior high school for blacks. The city boasted two colleges—William Marsh Rice Institute for the Advancement of Literature, Science, and Art (James A. Baker, President of Trustees) and St. Thomas College, a Catholic School. H. C. Schumacher was president of the Chamber of Commerce. Among the clubs were the Houston Left Hand Hunting and Fishing Club founded in 1887, J. L. Mitchell, Chief Shark. The Bender Hotel was a popular meeting place. The one public library was the Houston Lyceum and Carnegie Library at Travis and McKinney Avenue, where I found many of my first stories. Miss Martha Schnitzer was librarian.

Newspapers listed in 1915 were the *Houston Post* and the *Houston Chronicle*, dailies; the *Houston Telegram* and *La Paz*, weeklies. The Grand Central Depot on Washington Street and the Union Station on Crawford Street served several rail lines, and the Galveston–Houston Electric Railway, with its depot on Texas Avenue, ran several interurban cars to Galveston daily.

In the seventy-six years preceding 1915, Houston had grown from a village to a thriving metropolis. In seventy-plus subsequent years, it has become one of the largest cities in the nation, with a population of two million or three million depending on who tells it.

Although fifty miles from the Gulf of Mexico, Houston was always envisioned as a seaport. The first small steamboat to attempt to go up the bayou was the *Laura*, under Capt. T. W. Grayson, in January, 1837. In May of the same year, Houston became the capital of the Texas republic, and in June the "city" incorporated. The first steamer packet to make a voyage directly from New Orleans to Houston was the SS *Ogden*, under Captain Huniland, arriving August 15, 1849. Then, in 1876, the *Clinton*, the first ocean steamship to navigate Buffalo Bayou, docked at Clinton Avenue. These were the pioneer forerunners of ships that have sailed into the channel of what now is one of the South's busiest ports, visited by great ships from around the world. This was the proud city in which I was to spend some fifty years, watching it grow to a great metropolis and helping to record its progress.

8.

City Side at the *Houston Post*

I didn't really expect to find newsworthy or feature stories on every corner as I took the streetcar down to Main Street the first morning that I was a newspaper reporter. But the elation of being on the staff of the *Houston Post* had given me a new perspective. I walked along Main, seeing every corner, every pedestrian, every vehicle in a new light and with a personal interest. I had to find something to write about. I had to have something on Mr. Warner's desk that day!

The kind gods that look after innocents and imbeciles must have been on duty. As I reached the intersection of Main and Texas, one of the busiest corners, I saw a crowd gathering and heard laughter. I joined the crowd to see a very old black man struggling to make a balking mule cross Main. The mule was hitched to a light cart and was afraid of the traffic. He had stopped in his tracks, as if stuck in concrete, and nothing could induce him to move.

"Light a fire under him, Uncle." "Twist his tail!" "Don't you have some sugar lumps?" Curbside advice was freely given, as the crowd grew larger.

"Never mind, never mind now," the old man said softly. "He just afeared, that's all. He a good mule. There fella, let's go now."

But gentle slaps and soft words were forgotten as the brown mule suddenly showed his rebellion by sitting down, breaking a cart shaft. Boisterous laughter was suddenly silenced, as a sprightly little woman stepped to the cart and faced the crowd.

"Shame!" she cried. "Come help this poor man. Suppose this were *your* mule!"

A patrolman put an end to the little drama, moving the crowd along. With the help of two spectators, he got the man and his mule along their way. Not an earthshaking event but grist for my mill. I quickly got names and the details and rushed to the newspaper office.

It was a small but real triumph when I saw Mr. Warner jab my handwritten story on the desk sticker to his right. I had been impressed by the sharp, upright stickers, one on his left and one on his right, and was to learn that copy stuck on the right one appeared in next morning's paper. Copy put on the left-hand sticker was sent to department editors who might wish to incorporate some ideas from it into stories of their own.

As he stuck my mule story on the right-hand sticker, Mr. Warner didn't look at me or speak.

I didn't ask him any fool questions.

I did not mention my mule story to Dad Danforth and Lila, but next morning at the breakfast table Dad found it and read it to us. There was much laughter and congratulations.

"So you are launched on a great career, Bess," teased Dad, a printer and former editor of small-town newspapers. "Well, you'll have a lot of fun and many disappointments. But I can tell you one thing — you'll never get rich!"

Lila beamed at me in her quiet way. "She'll go a long way and write many worthwhile things. And who knows, she may write the Great American Novel and get rich!"

I knew I'd never lack the affection and backing of these two loyal friends, in success or failure. But there were no ifs or buts in my mind. I would not fail. I still can feel the thrill and satisfaction of that moment. It did not matter that my little feature had appeared on an inside page, almost hidden by advertisements bordering it. It did not matter that there was nothing to indicate I wrote it. *I* knew it. It was my brainchild — spread out for the world to read!

Over that weekend I searched diligently for more feature opportunities, haunting the Houston Public Library a few blocks from the *Post* building. The children's department was always a good source. I also made friends in schools nearby. There I ran into my first experiences with competitive reporters from other papers and, to my dismay, from a jealous reporter from my own paper. He was the school editor, and I had trespassed. In my ignorance, I did not know that reporters guard their assigned runs as holy ground.

Although I did not know it then, I am sure Mr. Warner often ran interference for me in such instances. So my brief stories appeared, albeit on page twenty with twelve-point heads, or even less conspicuously. Never mind. They landed on the right-hand sticker.

Each day I was learning more about the city, making new friends. I had known Ray Dudley, one of the reporters, when we were in Baylor University, and when he found I was trying out for work on the *Post,* he occasionally took me with him on his assignments. These were "open-sesame" experiences for me. He was a patient teacher.

I did worry though, as the days of my two weeks were going by, and nothing approaching a front-page creation came from my big black pencil. My check on my first Friday payday was six dollars. I was pretty low.

Then, on Monday of the second week, Mr. Warner called Ray Dudley into his office. From my table in the corner, I heard the conversation.

"The Southern Baptist Convention is coming here for five days, starting Wednesday," Mr. Warner told him. "This is the first time in twenty-five years it has met in Houston, and they expect hundreds of delegates and visitors. Tell Charlie to put somebody else on your run, and you take over this convention. Tell Charlie to give you somebody to help you." Charlie Maes was city editor.

I saw my opportunity.

"Let me help him, Mr. Warner!"

The keen eyes looked at me over the spectacles.

"What do you know about the Baptists?"

"Everything!" I answered. "I was bred and born a Baptist."

"She can do it, Mr. Warner," Ray backed me up calmly. "We were in Baylor together."

So, with no reporting experience, I turned in reams of copy on that convention, written in longhand, from early morning until midnight deadlines, doing interviews, personality sketches, features, women's meetings, and convention sessions, as assigned to me by Ray — a cram course in journalism if there ever was one.

On Friday payday, my check was eighteen dollars — seven dollars less than the average pay for the men! But I had won. I had learned to expect the unexpected from Mr. Warner, so was not surprised that our "deal" was never mentioned again. My fears were over. Now I truly had begun a career in communications that was to span over seventy years. I was the first woman to work on the city side of a Houston newspaper.

As the days passed, I practiced typing at Mr. Warner's old "mill" from early morning until he was due at 11:00 A.M. I started turning in typed copy. I also learned where and how to find feature stories and became bolder in seeking interviews. Ray, always interested and kind, gave me many tips for human interest stories growing out of his criminal courts run.

The first Friday in July was to be a red-letter day for me. I was sitting at the table in the corner of Mr. Warner's office when he came in at eleven o'clock. "Charlie wants to see you," he said offhandedly. Surprised, I walked across the city room to City Editor Maes's desk.

"Miss Whitehead, I have set this desk and typewriter here for you." He pointed to a desk near his own. "I want you to start today covering civil courts, as well as general news of the public library. You will need to be at the courthouse every day from one o'clock to four, then come back here and get your copy in by 5:30. Ray will go with you today and show you the ropes.

"Ask Miss Schnitzer, the librarian, for a schedule of the Library Board meetings and attend them as the *Post*'s representative. Continue to pick up news and features, and, by the way, turn in your copy to me from now on." He smiled as he handed me a card reading "Representing the Houston Post," with my name written on it and signed "Charles Maes, City Editor."

I managed to thank him quietly, but my heart was beating a happy rhythm as I gathered up my few belongings from Mr. Warner's corner table. He did not turn in his swivel chair, and I thanked him silently. Not only had I learned not to ask him any fool questions, I never made any fool comments, either.

Although I was proud to be "promoted" to the city room, I missed the intimate association I had enjoyed with the managing editor and his public from my grandstand seat at the corner table in his office. As I settled at my new desk, I recalled my amazement at the complaints, trivial or pathetic, that these visitors brought to the editor. After the first days of listening, I had written a little verse and put it on Mr. Warner's desk.

I didn't see the verse put on any sticker and supposed it had landed in "File 13" until a few days later, in Judd Mortimer Lewis's column "Tampering with Trifles," I read his introduction, "I found this pinned to my desk with a hat pin," and then the lines of my verse.

I had known for some time that the reporters in the city room were curious about the woman who sat in Mr. Warner's corner and was ambitious to join their ranks. I had talked briefly with a few of them, and they had mentioned my work with Ray. But I was wary of them. I knew I did not know how to handle any advances, so I tried to avoid them. Again, I was to learn this attitude seemed to challenge the men. Even reticent and sometimes fatherly Mr. Warner tested me, although I did not realize it at the time.

One Friday when the heat seemed more stifling than usual, he inquired, "Have you ever been to the Galveston beach? That's where we ought to be in weather like this." I had not and longed to go.

"How about meeting me here about ten Sunday morning? You must see the Gulf. Bring your bathing suit." I was delighted and agreed at once. It never occurred to me that there was any impropriety in going with him. He had told me about his two daughters, Ida Mae and Hallie, and his wife and little son. Why, he was an old man, old enough to be my father.

So Sunday morning, I went to the *Post* building early. Waiting for me were Mr. Warner—and Hallie. I was delighted to meet her. It was much later before I understood Mr. Warner's enigmatic smile. He must have thought, "Is she real?"

I hardly knew when I began to be accepted in the city room as a reporter rather than regarded as an interloper. Mr. Maes or Mr. Warner might have had something to do with it, but I like to think it was because I did my work quietly and efficiently. Anyway, I soon felt accepted and at ease.

Those were satisfying days. That which was routine to most reporters was new and exciting to me. I covered the civil courts routinely, but I expanded the little-noticed library run into a full Children's Page for Sunday editions. "Develop it any way you want—seems a good idea," Mr. Maes had answered to my suggestion. In addition to stories of children's books, library activities, and a little school news, I wrote original verses and ran series of articles called "Children of History." Then in August, as a "cub" of only four months, a love for my work, a "nose for news," and circumstances combined to bring to me the most incredible true-life feature story of my long career and one any reporter would consider a bonanza beyond price. It also brought me my first byline.

It was a full-page story of the tragic ordeal of Minnie Florea, a sixteen-year-old girl who saw her mother, father, two sisters, and a brother perish in the great tidal wave disaster that hit Galveston Island on August 15, 1915.

Briefly, John C. Florea, editor and publisher of the Richmond, Texas, *Coaster,* and his family and other relatives were vacationing at Surfside on Galveston Bay near Velasco when storm warnings were issued. False reports regarding the force and direction of the storm persuaded some of the group, including the Florea family, to discount the danger and to wait too long to leave the area. They took refuge in a lighthouse, along with others, twenty-three in all, including three lifeguards. Of the twenty-three, only Minnie and the lifeguards survived.

As the lighthouse crumbled under the waves and wind, Minnie saw her father and small sister's lifeboat capsize, her brother dive into oil-coated water and never rise again, her sister carried out to sea, and her mother turn loose of rafters, saying she wanted to join her husband.

"I held to whatever I could grab," Minnie told me three weeks afterward, "a life belt, planks from the lighthouse wreck, the lid of a cedar chest, and many times just *nothing.* I could not give up. All my family had gone to heaven. The Bible says a suicide will not go to heaven, so I could not suicide. I had to pray and hold on."

Hold on she did, for thirty-three hours, never knowing whether she was being borne out to sea or shoreward, her face almost a solid blister. Finally, she felt flotsam and sand under her feet. But even when she knew she was near the shore, her paralyzed legs would not function. She finally crawled to a lighted house, far on the east beach. There she was taken in, warmed, and fed, and found that the lifeguards had been carried by the waves to the same refuge.

Through friends, I learned about the girl, who was then in a Galveston hospital. I took my tip to Mr. Warner. He located Minnie's aunt, who lived in Houston. I called on her, and she promised she would shield the girl from opposition reporters. When Minnie was brought to her house and was well enough for an interview, she was true to her word. I spent an entire morning talking to Minnie, listening to her incredible story.

Minnie Florea was "adopted" by the Texas Press Association meeting in convention in June, 1916, in El Paso. The resolution, adopted unanimously, preserved in the minutes of the convention, is a classic of the flowery but sincere nomenclature of seventy years ago. The Association helped her enter Rice Institute. In time, she graduated and became a teacher. The resolution, compiled by James H. Lowry of the *Honey Grove Signal* for the minutes of the TPA meeting is quoted here in part:

One year ago in Corpus Christ By-the-Sea (at the annual meeting) there was with us a maiden with eyes as blue as the fairy flax and cheeks like the dawn of day, whose silvery laughter rippled as sun-kissed waves on the shining strand, a maiden who played with us and made our hearts glad with her gay youth. Some two short months passed and the Grim Reaper, whose name is Death, came with his sickle keen, and reaped the bearded grain at a breath, and when the storm was over, this little maid was left to tread the wine press of life alone. Because we, too, loved her beloved loved ones, now awaiting us in the fields of light above; because we feel somehow their everlasting peace will be intensified by this action, because we love this maid as one of us and desire to keep her and be of comfort and service to her through all the years that are to be, therefore be it RESOLVED that we, the *Texas Press Association,* adopt Miss Minnie Florea as our beloved daughter, loving and cherishing her to the best of our ability, as would her own sainted father and mother.

Much later, as the sixtieth anniversary of the destructive storm surge of 1915 approached, I wrote Minnie, then living in retirement with her husband of many years, asking for an interivew by telephone and a letter for a follow-up story on her ordeal. She answered:

Do forgive me when I tell you I could not deliberately open Pandora's box and bring back to consciousness my loss of so long ago. An occasional nightmare still throws me into an emotional upset. Aside from that sealed off part of my life, I have been so normal, fortunate and happy, there isn't any further story. I hope you can understand because your interest is really appreciated.

She signed her married name, which I have never divulged. Although I had enough data, and her letter, to make an interesting story, I never pursued it.

The elation and satisfaction I felt in seeing this great feature story in print so early in my career were not rooted primarily in a feeling of ego. Of course, I viewed the story with pride. But it meant much more, hard to define. It was a reassurance that step by step my lifetime goal was accessible, although my reach would not exceed my grasp.

9.

Dallas

That autumn of 1915 was a busy one. Although the war in Europe accelerated and was viewed with more and more anxiety in America, holiday festivities followed custom, and my Children's Page flourished. Many small readers wrote to the *Post,* and their letters were featured. At that time, it never occurred to me that this was one of the best advertising and subscription promotions of the paper.

One day in early January of 1916, Mr. Warner called me into his office. "We are going to start a joint project with the Queen picture show that will be right down your alley," he told me. "Saturday morning shows for kids. I want you to go to the Queen Theatre. Do you know where it is?"

"Yes sir, on Main between Texas and Preston."

"Right. I guess you are a Houstonian now. Well, go see Bill McDonald in his office upstairs above the Queen. He has a lot of dope on kids' pictures, and he will give you the dates for the shows. You are to write advance notices that the *Post* will run Thursdays, Fridays, and Saturdays. I don't care how you write the stories—just make them appealing to kids. Bring your copy to me."

"Will a *Chronicle* reporter be there?"

"Of course not, this is the *Post*'s baby!"

I felt squelched, but didn't ask any more fool questions. This was my introduction to newspaper promotions.

All right. A new challenge. I loved the movies. But I'd never seen any aimed at children. Wonder what they could be?

I soon found out. *Keystone Cops, Rumpelstiltskin, The Old Woman Who Lived in a Shoe.* A new world to me. Make them appeal to the kids, the boss said. How could I do that?

I carried a stack of publicity clip sheets back to my desk and read them with a purpose. Mr. McDonald had told me to be at the Queen at nine the next morning when one of the films would be previewed.

But now I must plan a way to "appeal to kids." I took the assignment seriously and over the weekend asked Lila for suggestions on how to approach it.

"Why not pretend it is the Fairy Lady writing as you tell the kids the Queen Theatre will be a fairyland on Saturday?" Just the thing. I had stories for the first three days on Mr. Warner's desk before he came in that Monday. I told the youngsters that my crew of little fairies was busy cleaning every corner of the Queen, arranging the music, and oiling the curtains that would be pulled back as the funny Keystone Cops came to visit them. Each day, the stories pictured a little more vividly the hilarious antics of the cops, the daring exploits of the pictures' heroines. The stories were signed "The Fairy Lady."

True to form, Mr. Warner made no comment. On Thursday the first story ran, unaltered, in a prominent box on page one. Heading the stories, in parentheses, were an introduction giving the hour of showing, 10:00 A.M., the promise of new pictures each Saturday, and a line naming the *Post* and Queen Theatre as sponsors. The other stories ran Friday and Saturday in front-page boxes.

By 9:00 A.M. Saturday, the sidewalk at the Queen was so blocked the theater doors had to be opened. By 9:15, every seat, downstairs and up, was taken and children, large and small, were sitting on the stairs, hanging on the box rails, and standing along the walls. So noisy was the clamor of the hundreds of children that the show had to start at 9:30.

By the next week, two matinees had to be run, one at 9:00 and one at 10:00 A.M. Chairs were borrowed from Vick's Ice Cream Parlor next door. Children by the dozens wrote letters each week to the Fairy Lady at the *Houston Post*. I used them in the advance stories.

By the fourth week, children had to be turned away, but each of them was given a free ice cream cone at Vick's. Still no comment from Mr. Warner. "He could give me a little credit," I complained to Dad and Lila.

"Hit him up for more salary," said Dad. I shrank from the idea.

"He knows what you are doing," advised Lila. "Don't push." Next weekend my check was for twenty-five dollars. Few men reporters got more.

My days were full now. Library Board meetings and news from

Miss Schnitzer's office added to my run. Bylines came very occasionally. I still lived with Lila, but had been paying my way since my
salary was eighteen dollars. It was a matter of pride to all of us that
I was making my way in the world of my choice. Secretly, my thoughts
began to turn to New York, Los Angeles, maybe Hollywood! I never
wanted to be an editor. I wanted to be the *best* of reporters and writers. But I also dreamed of new worlds to conquer.

Spring was in the air that early April morning of 1916 when Mr.
Warner sent for me. "I want you to be here at my office at one o'clock
sharp to go to lunch on the Rice Roof." He swivelled toward his
desk, adding over his shoulder, "I mean *one o'clock.*"

I was curious but seldom surprised at anything the eccentric editor did now. I felt he was my friend and knew he kept up with my
work as he did that of all the reporters. But although I was "Bess"
to most of the reporters and to Charlie Maes, Mr. Warner and I
stayed on a last-name basis.

The Rice Hotel Roof Garden? Pretty swanky place. I was wearing a light coat suit with pullover sweater. I'd have time to go home
and change to a fresh blouse. I hurried at once to our apartment
on La Branch and back, and at exactly one o'clock I was standing
in Mr. Warner's door.

We walked silently down the fourth-floor corridor and took the
elevator. Not until we reached the entrance to the hotel across the
street and down a block did he stop and turn to me.

"We are meeting Bill McDonald on the roof, and E. H. Hulsey
from Dallas. Hulsey owns the Queen Theatre and Zoe Theatre here.
He also owns theaters in Dallas, Galveston, Waco, and in other towns
in Texas and Oklahoma. He is going to offer you a job."

"Why?" I asked in astonishment.

"Because he likes the way you publicize the kid matinees. He wants
you to start them in many of his other theaters."

I was dismayed at the thought. Leave the *Post?* Leave Houston?
Leave Lila? Leave Mr. Warner? He laughed at the reaction that must
have been mirrored in my face.

"Aren't you flattered? He gives you credit for the smashing success
of the kid matinees. He will probably pay you a good deal more money
than the *Post* can."

I questioned him with my eyes. I wanted to say "Do you want me to?" A fool question, maybe. I asked it diffidently.

"Do you advise me to go, Mr. Warner?"

He put his hand on my shoulder and paid me the first compliment in words in the year I had known him.

"Bess Whitehead, I'll say this to you: you've shown more potential for a newspaper career than any reporter I've known in my thirty years in this work. But your hearing defect will always bar you from the top. With moving picture promotions you can go far."

Pictures in 1916 were silent.

We stood in silence.

"Cheer up, you don't have to go! I'm not firing you. But maybe you'd like to try a new field. I guarantee you can always come back."

He took my arm and led me to the elevator.

"Which is your 'good' ear?" The right one, I told him as we reached the roof and saw two men waiting. After introductions, Mr. Warner quietly steered me to a seat on the left of Mr. Hulsey.

The Dallas man was affable, quick spoken. He complimented me, Mr. Warner, and his Queen manager on what he termed the phenomenal success of the kid matinees and the goodwill he felt they created in the community.

"This has proved to be great promotional idea, Warner's idea. I want to try it in other places." He turned to me. "I told Warner I want to steal you from him. How would you like to travel for the Hulsey theaters for a while, then live in Dallas?"

I was thankful Mr. Warner had forewarned me, and I could meet his questions with some composure. As Mr. Hulsey enlarged on his plans, I saw that Mr. Warner had tactfully engaged Mr. McDonald in other subjects. Knowing him, though, I felt he was not missing a word of our give and take. Mr. Hulsey told me of his other theaters, talked of the towns they were in, told me he was negotiating for a vaudeville house in Dallas, and for other movie theaters in Arkansas.

He spoke of the Hulsey offices in the Old Mill Theatre in Dallas; of Herschel Stuart, his general manager; Buddy Stuart, his Old Mill manager; of Lorena, the organist there who was a favorite of everybody, someone I would enjoy knowing, he said. When he finally lowered his voice and asked me what salary I was getting at the *Post*, intuition rather than experience cautioned me. We sparred a few minutes, then with a smile, he dropped the question.

"I can offer you fifty dollars a week and all traveling expenses paid while you are on the road. Then when you come to Dallas to stay, we will see just what your work will be. I'd like to start a little movie magazine to give away at the door of the Old Mill. If we can start that and you can handle it, I can pay you more."

I wanted desperately to look at Mr. Warner but did not.

"That is a very generous offer, Mr. Hulsey," I heard myself saying. "But I'll have to have a little time to think about it and talk to my family."

"Of course," he agreed. "I'm on my way to Galveston and our theater there. I'll be back through Houston in three days. You make up your mind, and I'll see you then."

When we left the Rice Hotel after lunch, Mr. Warner and I again walked across Texas Avenue in silence. At the *Post*'s corner he turned toward Billy McKinnon's restaurant, a favorite coffee hangout for *Post* and *Chronicle* newsmen.

"I noticed how you would not tell Hulsey your *Post* salary," his eyes twinkled.

"You know, he offered me twice as much." I was still surprised.

"Yes, I know. Well, talk to your friend Lila, then make up your own mind."

I turned toward Bush and Gerts Piano Company, a few blocks away where Lila worked as a secretary. Soon I was almost running. My news couldn't wait.

"You will go," said Lila after she heard me out. As I looked into her calm eyes, the understanding that always passed between us and needed no words, sealed my decision.

As I looked back in my mind to this May in 1916 when I was preparing to leave the *Post,* I realized how I had grown in experience, objectivity, and emotional stability. My contact with shrewd and knowledgeable co-workers and with a public I liked but now viewed with a more factual outlook, had brought me confidence. The guidance, however brusque and seemingly stern, of Harry Warner had been a real education for me. Sudden tears filled my eyes as I thought of him with appreciation and affection.

Harry Warner left the *Post* a few years later, buying the daily paper in Paris, Texas, where he died many years later. I treasure a letter from him written in 1917 explaining that his seeming harshness with me as a "cub" was to "toughen" me up, and also, a letter written to my baby girl, Lila Bess, born in Denver in 1920, in which he said, "Your mother will bear acquaintance. You will find her set in her ways, but she can be argued out of them on a reasonable basis."

Even as I felt sad at leaving my beloved *Houston Post* and friends, I looked forward eagerly to my new home, new associates, and new writing experiences. The glamour of the movie world was exciting, too. Threats of war seemed unreal.

Maybe *this* was the path to Hollywood!

It was more than a physical change from Houston to Dallas. I missed the semitropical temperatures of the coast, the winding bayous, the great trees, flowering shrubs, and evergreens. The bare prairies that I saw from my train windows as I neared Dallas looked unfriendly, very unlike the warmth of the Gulf country. But as I stepped from the train to be greeted by Mr. Hulsey himself and his general manager, Herschel Stuart, all the promise of a new and exciting adventure buoyed my spirits.

It was early afternoon, and I had eaten only toast and coffee for breakfast on the train. The delicious lunch we shared at the plush Adolphus Hotel and the friendly get-together session were an auspicious beginning for the years I was to spend with the Hulsey Theatres.

My temporary home that had been arranged at the Adolphus was also a new experience. I was to live there "a week or so while you get acquainted with us and prepare to travel," Mr. Hulsey told me. I was to sign tabs for meals and other expenses. Luxury! A huge basket of fruit and spring flowers in my room helped to dim my first impressions of Dallas's narrow streets with tangled traffic, few trees barely budding, and lack of flowers. I had left Houston bright with azaleas, hedges of evergreens, and glossy magnolia trees.

The theater offices were over the Old Mill Theatre on Elm Street. Other theaters of the chain were the Queen, a first-run movie house, two second-runs, and the Hippodrome, which showed five acts of vaudeville and a newsreel each week. I walked from the Adolphus to the Old Mill after breakfast. Here I was greeted by Buddy Stuart, Herschel's brother, with whom I was to work in the advertising department. I was assigned a small office, an executive desk, and a sparkling new Underwood typewriter, a far cry from the knife-carved, cigarette-burned desk and tired Royal typewriter that had been my domain at the *Post*. I was impressed but smothered a brief nostalgia for the noisy city room and the reporters' sprightly repartee.

Mr. Hulsey lost no time in briefing me on the itinerary I was to follow in establishing the kid matinees in his theaters in Texas, Oklahoma, and Arkansas. We began with the Queen in Dallas. Following the plan used in Houston, I was to contact prominent women's club leaders in each city and enlist their backing of our proposed Saturday morning entertainment for children. The theater managers in each place would line up the local newspaper as cosponsor, a sure goodwill promotion. I wrote the publicity material in advance, using quotes of approval from the women.

Usually an ice cream parlor or a candy shop would tie into the promotion by advertising special treats after the show. Children's movie favorites of the day were Mary Pickford, Marguerite Clark, Charlie Chaplin, and other comedians. Without exception, we had to schedule two shows in every place to accommodate the crowds. Group photographs were run in the local papers each week. Many merchants selling children's clothes, bicycles, and other toys advertised specialties following the matinees.

I became an experienced traveler and public relations contact, enjoying every minute of the new job. By the end of that summer, we had kid matinees well established throughout the Hulsey chain. In September, I returned to my office at the Old Mill. I wrote advance publicity stories for the local theaters and mailed copies to all the out-of-town theaters to be placed in local papers as their schedules permitted. I also helped Buddy Stuart write ads. This young man never quite accepted a woman as coworker. We were never close friends, but we got along. Lorena, the Old Mill organist who was the sweetheart of everybody, especially Herschel, who wooed her without success, became my friend. We were the only women on the staff except for a series of secretaries who were lured by the glamour of the theater but left because the demanding office work was far from glamorous.

In my work I had discovered the movie magazines, which at that time seldom indulged in the belittling gossip, jealousies, and intrigue that fill today's Hollywood publications. I outlined a "movieland" magazine I thought the Hulsey Theatres might publish as a give-away to patrons. Mr. Hulsey and Herschel liked the idea, and in a few weeks the eight-page, 8½-by-11–inch magazine *Movieland,* which I designed, wrote, and edited, began appearing and was given away to patrons. It was an immediate success. It was issued monthly and carried the scheduled showings in each of the Dallas houses and stories about the stars, other players, plots, backgrounds, and word portraits of Hollywood personalities. In those days, producers, stars, and ex-hibitors conspired to keep the marriages or families of stars secret. The idea was to always present them as alluring romantic singles, desirable but unattainable!

The front and back covers of *Movieland* were printed in red and black, and the back page was sold to advertisers. This big ad was usually written by Herschel Stuart, but occasionally he would ask me to write it. And thereby hangs a tale—embarrassing to me but a valuable lesson.

The King Candy Company of Fort Worth bought the back page of *Movieland* one month and sent us a photograph of a beautiful box of candy. As Mary Pickford was a great favorite of mine, I spent a happy half day designing an ad in which I juxtaposed the photo of the lovely candy box and a popular photograph of Mary Pickford with her famous long blond curls. The big headline read "Sweets to the Sweet."

No one edited my work, so the ad showed up in the next *Movie-land.* It was colorful and attractive. I was proud of it—until a week later. Mr. Hulsey called me in his office to read a letter from Miss Pickford's agent. It was a kind but firm admonition that the un-authorized use of the star's picture to advertise a product was grounds for a court suit. I was much relieved as the letter continued: "How-ever, we believe that in this case there was no intent to misuse this material. Please be advised that any future unauthorized use of pic-tures of or quotes from Miss Pickford will not be overlooked."

Of course, the King Candy Company had no complaints. Mr. Hulsey was kind, too. He never referred to the matter again and continued to give me a free rein.

But despite the satisfactions and exhilaration of my job, certainty of American involvement in Europe was depressing. War rumors increased, and war stories filled the papers and the newsreels.

An air of expectancy and dread colored our days. My friend Lila came to Dallas as Mr. Hulsey's secretary. I had been living with a dear old couple whom I had met through a cousin, but I moved with Lila into a boardinghouse on Maple Street in the Oak Lawn Addition.

Oak Lawn, an area near downtown Dallas, had at one time been a section of fine homes, but in 1916 was succumbing to progress and an exodus to the suburbs. Many of the large homes became boardinghouses, a living accommodation now almost obsolete. Lila and I rented a large second-story room with windows opening onto a screened porch. We were served a hearty breakfast and evening meal each day for which we each paid thirty dollars a month. After we had proved good-paying tenants for two months, our landlady furnished us with a second dresser. We were reminded of our college days and were happy to be together.

There were other boarders in the house, several of them men and most of them on the second floor. My reticent friend Lila kept a small handgun in her room, often in her purse, and always under her pillow at night. That summer when the heat was suffocating, we got permission to put our double bed on the porch and climbed back and forth from our room through a window. One night I was awakened gradually by a gentle and repeated squeezing of my arm and leg. As I became aware of the rhythmic pressure, I realized Lila was warning me to be quiet. When I finally squeezed her arm to let her know I was awake, she spoke.

"You are standing in the doorway and I see you clearly," she said calmly. "I have a pistol in my hand, pointed at you, and it is loaded."

"Don't shoot, lady!" a man's alarmed voice answered. "I just came out to get cool, and I didn't know anybody was out here." His voice trailed off as he beat a hasty retreat. Our alarm clock said it was 4:00 A.M. There was much giggling after that but not much sleep.

Another incident from those days centered around a beautiful suit in a shop window that we passed daily on our way to work. It was made of pure corded silk and was a heavenly blue that I loved. I longed to own that suit, but the twenty-five-dollar price plainly marked on a card at the model's foot was discouraging. I could not afford it.

After a few days we were delighted to read a new card: "Reduced to $20."

"I'll help you, and maybe they will let us pay it out by the week," said my loyal Lila. "You ought to have it; it's just the blue of your eyes."

But I told the devil to get behind me and resisted temptation. A few days later the card read: "Reduced to $15."

"Maybe something is wrong with it," I argued, and still resisted. Pretty summer frocks began to fill the window, and the hot weather melted away most suit displays. But the blue suit stayed in the window, and when it was marked down to $12.50 I bought it. It was perfect, no flaws in it, and it really did bring out the blue in my eyes. I loved it.

A few evenings later when we decided to splurge on a steak dinner downtown, I wore my new suit. As I reached for my favorite dish of okra pickled in vinegar, the dish tilted and, alas, the stringent liquid spilled squarely on the lap of my beautiful blue skirt. We were never able to get the spot out, nor could a professional cleaner restore the color. Finally, I had the suit dyed black and wore it for several years. When I wrote my mother about the "tragedy" she responded: "Pride goeth before a fall."

As the New Year of 1917 came in, an era of peaceful and leisurely living ended forever. Army and Navy reserves were being activated. Loudspeakers blared news in public places, and war hysteria was increasing. On February 3, 1917, the United States broke relations with Germany after U.S. merchant ships carrying supplies to Great Britain were torpedoed. When Congress refused to arm the merchant ships, President Woodrow Wilson did so by executive order. Then our government intercepted a note from Germany to Mexico, asking Mexico to enter the war against the United States and fight to take U.S. territories in the United States, including Texas. On April 6, 1917, the United States declared war on Germany, adopted selective conscription, and on June 26 sent the first American Expeditionary Force to France. For the first time in many years, the United States was at war.

In our little world in Dallas, war films continued to fill our theater screens. Crowds flocked to see and applaud them and to see the newsreels depicting the excitement, the black humor, and the tragedies of war. My work expanded. I was often asked to speak to school groups and adult clubs about how the war films were made and how Hollywood personalities were responding to the drives to sell war bonds and war stamps.

Our theater audiences grew. Mr. Hulsey was quick to see the value of the goodwill gestures we made through my talks to various groups and the pages of *Movieland*. He lent films to school groups and made many talks himself to men's clubs and patriotic gatherings. All this was good for business, but E. H. Hulsey's first motives were patriotic. He is long since gone, but he was a loyal Dallasite and caring American, a kind man, a concerned and appreciative employer, and a loyal friend.

In May of 1917, as army cantonments and training fields for flyers opened up in Dallas and Fort Worth, quiet and unassuming Lila gave us a real shock. She resigned to enter a small flying school that opened in Marlin, Texas. She suited herself with custom-made brown corduroy flying suits and entered the school with three other students, against the alarmed protests of her father.

"Babe," he wrote me in dismay, "has lost her mind. Those chicken crate planes in Marlin will kill her. Can't you do something to stop her?"

I didn't have to try. When the only other woman student and her instructor fell to their deaths and Dad suffered a heart attack, Lila packed her pretty suit and returned to her typewriter. Years later when my young daughter, looking at a photograph of Lila as an aviatrix in training, said, "Why did you quit, Aunt Lila? You might have been an Amelia Earhart!" Lila smiled. "It was a sweet dream," she said pensively.

Even before Lila went to flying school, I was corresponding with pen pals I had made in Hollywood, especially Miss Loyola O'Connor, a character actress well known through David Griffith films. She and her sister lived in a cozy little home in the Hollywood Hills. I confided to her my ambition to go to Hollywood, not as an actress, but as a scenario writer. She invited me to try my luck and to stay with her until I found whether I could make it or not—"as our guest," she wrote. She offered to arrange an interview for me with the personnel manager of the Griffith Studios.

I loved my job in Dallas and hesitated to leave. Mr. Hulsey gave me three months' leave and assured me I could return if things did not pan out. He was as good as his word, and when I left his employ in 1918, he wrote: "I have appreciated you as an employee. You are a talented young woman and a person of rare integrity. I wish for you success and happiness in whatever you wish to be."

There was another situation that threatened my dream of going to Hollywood. Hal, the debonair Baylor sweetheart, showed up with all his old charm and began to court me again. He said the coming of war had brushed aside the years we had not seen each other, that he had long known I was the only girl he really loved. He had joined the naval air force and would leave in a few weeks for the Seattle training base. He proposed we get married before he had to leave. Although the old affection was aroused, I resisted. I would not give up my Hollywood dream.

10.

Hollywood Interlude

I was thrilled that I was going to Hollywood to try my luck at writing scenarios. I also was thrilled by the prospect of the long train ride from Dallas to Los Angeles. I liked trains and was looking forward to a leisurely trip. Furthermore, I knew all trains were crowded with servicemen, who were an additional attraction. These men, like our "tea dance" partners at the Adolphus Hotel in Dallas, were with very few exceptions friendly and appreciative of the opportunity to meet "nice girls," and jolly companions. To hear these men, many of them very young, tell of their homes and families in faraway states, and to help them forget homesickness was a happy experience. I knew I'd meet more of these men from all over the United States on the train.

The car was full when I stepped aboard at 8:00 A.M., mostly women with babies, several of them crying. But at the far end of the car was a group of servicemen, some standing, a few seated. As I waited at the entrance with my overnight bag in my hand, two of them stood up and one walked quickly down the aisle to escort me to his vacant seat.

"Here, lady," he said, "come sit with us. We can't offer you a concert, but we can a seat!"

"Now, was that nice?" I chided as he took my bag. "These little folks are tired and bored."

"No," he smiled, "it wasn't but, you know, we are tired and bored too!"

When I found they were alternating with the one seat, I told them I'd join them if I was counted in the game too. That called for a round of Cokes and as the train went slowly on the way I learned that some of the men had been traveling for twelve to twenty-four hours with no rest. I also learned that the women with children were on the way to spend a few hours with husbands who were being shipped out or returning from such a visit. No one had Pullman reservations. I did but was asked to spend each day in the chair car while someone else slept in my berth. When I was escorted to a berth the first night, I persuaded a very young mother with a baby and a two-year-old to take my place. With a big pillow, I did very well in her seat, especially as the servicemen visited with me until the wee hours. The three-day trip to Los Angeles was stressful but never boring.

This was typical of travel during World War I. Gasoline was rationed for car travel. Roads were not good in many areas, and existing highways were crowded with army trucks packed to the limit with troops.

Still excited by the three-day train ride from Dallas, I took a cab to Miss O'Connor's home. She and her sister greeted me cordially. Then, over a cup of tea, she gave me a shocking piece of news.

"My dear," said my gracious gray-haired hostess, "I do not want you to be too upset, but I have to tell you that the Griffith Studios were closed while you were on your way out here, and the whole business is in a state of uncertainty."

She could see my dismay. "Let's look at it this way. We will try Universal Studio, the Tom Ince, and others, and you have a home with us as long as you wish to stay. If things work out for you, well and good. If not, you will have had a fine vacation and will meet many Hollywood people and go to many new places. Doesn't that sound better?"

Of course it did, and how lucky I was to have such a friend. We did make connections with the Tom Ince studios at Culver City, and I was at work in their public relations department within a week. Thomas Ince had opened his studio a short time before and was adding many types of stories to his well-known western dramas. Lack of financing would cause the studio to be sold in 1918 to another producer just becoming prominent, Samuel Goldwyn. But, Ince would go on to make his most successful film, *Anna Christie,* starring one of Griffith's stars, Blanche Sweet.

Miss O'Connor proved a real friend during the short time I was in the film colony. She never tired of telling me of the colorful history of this Cahuenga Valley, where the little pueblo of San Angelo and its glamorous subdivision seven miles west started. She had suggested to David Griffith a drama based on this history: the bringing in of camels by a character known as "Greek George" to open a wagon road from Mexico to California; the exploits of early desperados, especially one Tiburcio Valdez; and other dramatic events, including a final triumph of the "good guys" (pioneer ranchers) over the "bad guys." She said Griffith was intrigued by the possibility of photographic backgrounds of the hills and valleys, the stirring action, and the battles he so loved to put on film. But financial troubles and competition from the other companies had forced him to put this and other film ventures on hold.

One interesting story Miss O'Connor told me as we took a sightseeing drive along a valley highway that had once been a winding cattle and sheep trail was how Hollywood got its name. When the wife of a real estate pioneer, Daeida Wilcox, was going east by train, a fellow traveler told about her home, which she had named Hollywood. When the real estate promoter's wife returned to California, she dubbed their 120-acre ranch Hollywood, "a pretty name." Later, when her husband filed a map of their property in the county records with a view to subdividing it, the name he put on the map was "Hollywood."

The Hollywood of 1917 was a part of Los Angeles, having been annexed in 1910. The area already had modern schools, churches, and libraries and was a thriving, successful community aside from the film-making businesses. The Women's Club had for years been an influential force in its goal of improving its social, intellectual, and cultural life. Some of the most impressive mansions then in Hollywood were built by pioneer citizens long before the rising film stars began to pepper the hills and canyons with their great estates, some ostentatious, others elegant and graceful.

It also was of special interest to me that it was a Texan, Charles Edward Toberman, an Aggie from Texas A&M College, who was making a success in the real estate and insurance business in Hollywood. People I met at the studios were apt to say, "You're from Texas—do you know Mr. Toberman?" In the next sixty years, he was to have an amazing career; and after building the famous Chinese Theatre, he would be widely known as "Mr. Hollywood."

In 1917, all the pictures were still silent, and David Griffith was the best-known director. However, others were coming from the East whose names were to become as well known: Laemmle, DeMille, Larky, Goldfish (later Goldman), Ince, Sennet, and Zukor. And in addition to Griffith's Biograph, there were other studios such as Selig, Vitagraph, Paramount, Triangle, Nestor, and Quality. Some had started in the East and then moved to the ideal climate of the West Coast.

Actors and actresses came from all parts of the nation, with many of the actresses finding a home at the "Studio Club." One of these was Zazu Pitts, whom Miss O'Connor had taken under her wing. When I met her, I found her a very quiet, even shy, young woman, much unlike her screen character.

The assaults on the studios by young stage-struck girls had begun before the Hollywood Chamber of Commerce began running ads to warn these aspirants and others attracted by the high wages: "Out of 100,000 Persons Who Started at the Bottom of the Screen's Ladder of Fame ONLY FIVE PERCENT REACH THE TOP."

But the growth of Hollywood did not depend on the studios alone. In ten years, from 1910 to 1920, its population increased by over 30,000. Ten years later, it had jumped to nearly 160,000. Real estate, oil, the wonderful California climate, and Pacific beaches brought all kinds of people to the area, who established the usual schools, churches, clubs, and all the refinements and necessities of a solid community. Choice residential property sold for as high as $10,000 an acre.

Dear Miss O'Connor. She had been one of my most inspiring pen pals for several years. She and her sister, also a character actress, had reached an age and a time in their careers when they could accept or refuse roles as they wished. Two of the most notable movies in which Loyola O'Connor played were *Birth of a Nation* and *Intolerance,* filmed after I left Hollywood. The last letter I received from her, some six years after I left Hollywood, was an unfinished one, with a note from her sister. Miss O'Connor had died in her sleep.

When I started work in Culver City that summer of 1917, I left the O'Connor home and rented a room near my work. It was in a quiet neighborhood in the home of Mr. and Mrs. Ben Foster. The first night I did not see or hear anyone when I came from work. I felt the strangeness of a new place, but I put my travel clock on the bedside table and soon went to sleep. Suddenly, I was wide awake. My bed was shaking eerily. I sat up, frozen with fear. Someone was under my bed!

It was pitch dark and I could not hear a sound. Should I call the Fosters? No! But I had to get out of that room. How could I get out of bed without that Someone under the bed grabbing my legs? Now, be reasonable, I told myself. I tried to slow my racing heart. Now, let's see . . . if I hold the headboard and stand up, I can jump almost to the door. As I started this maneuver, the bed suddenly stopped shaking. I slipped down onto the pillows and my common sense took over. An earthquake! I felt foolish, but I did look under the bed! I would experience more of these, common to the West Coast, and I never failed to tremble along with the earth.

At the studios, I had been assigned a desk and introduced to the writer at the adjacent desk. At the time, her name meant nothing to me. But Adela Rogers St. John was an influential Hollywood writer and well-known reporter on the *Los Angeles Herald.* I remember her as a gracious lady, kind to a newcomer.

I wrote publicity tearsheets about the studio productions that were sent to moving picture exhibitors throughout the country. While in Dallas, I had received these blurbs regularly and placed them in the local papers. They were filled with reviews of the Ince films, stories of stars, unusual locations, and stunt performers. I was adept at this kind of writing. Several of them went to my friend Herman Philipson at the *Dallas Times Herald.* He asked me for other short items for a daily movie column and ran a head picture of me with them. One of the few times I was a "columnist."

One of the interviews that the *Times Herald* used was with Wallace Reid, a handsome leading man in silent films. It was the result of a chance encounter as I walked across the studio lot. I saw a man's legs extending from under an automobile as he worked on its underside, and I stooped to ask directions. He crawled from under the car, his smiling face marked with grease.

"You're new around here, aren't you?" I stammered a reply when I recognized him. He wiped his hands and forehead with a greasy rag and sat on the car fender. "It's hot," he said. "Sit down and rest a minute." So sitting on the fender, we exchanged information about ourselves. He was interested when he found I was writing publicity. "Well, tell the folks I may not be so hot an actor, but I'm a good mechanic." He knew he was one of the most popular stars of the time. I found him to be a friendly, unpretentious young man. I felt I had lost a personal friend when he became one of the first victims of the drug excesses of Hollywood.

Most silent films were two-reelers. I had told the personnel manager, Mr. Abel, it was my ambition to write scenarios. After I had been with the studios one month, I was asked to try my hand at this. I was given short stories and told to put them in scenario form. When I turned in my assignments, I ventured to enclose original stories, also in scenario form. The manager of the publicity group congratulated me and suggested I write others. I wrote *A Georgia Peach* with Douglas Fairbanks, Sr., in mind and a children's story for Marguerite Clark, who, although an adult, played in many fairy stories, including *Snow White*. Mr. Abel accepted everything I turned in without comment. I watched the bulletin board where stories approved for production were listed. Mine were never posted, but my weekly salary was raised from thirty-five to fifty dollars. Adela encouraged me to write stories with Texas backgrounds.

Miss O'Conner kept in touch also. "Patience," she advised me. "The mills of the gods grind slowly. I know they will grind exceedingly fine for you." Patience had never been one of my traits. I needed more solid assurance. Of course, I was a little homesick, and this was made more acute by the letters and telegrams Hal was sending me almost daily, urging me to return to Dallas and marry him before he had to leave for war. His time was short. But I wanted very much to justify my coming to Hollywood and my friends' confidence in my ability to succeed. I was not a quitter—I would try harder.

Almost every evening during this time in Hollywood, I went to rallies in parks and downtown Los Angeles, where name stars and others sold war bonds and war stamps. Many of these drew enormous crowds, all emotionally stirred because of war time. News of the U.S. forces, now in battle in Europe, was broadcast at every meeting. Patriotic speeches were applauded wildly, and often the reactions approached frenzy. It was a time of high tension and emotion, but as yet not accompanied by violence.

One night in downtown Los Angeles, in one of those pretty little parks that cover one square, with beautiful California flowers and shrubs planted along gravel paths leading to a central water fountain and pool, there had been built a temporary stage. Charlie Chaplin and Douglas Fairbanks, Sr., were scheduled to lead a bevy of movie stars selling bonds. Many large trees were on the rim of the park, and the stage was beside a big, spreading pepper tree.

A large audience around the stage completely disregarded the flowers and shrubs, trampling them under foot like so many weeds. Some climbed into the trees, and children stood on grownups' shoulders. Fairbanks and Chaplin really put on a show, each trying to outsell the other on bonds. They announced that the one who sold the smallest amount of bonds would give his personal check for a thousand dollars. Adding to the fun and the noise, an "orchestra" on the back of the stage played raucous tunes. It was a comb-and-paper orchestra led by Harold Lloyd. The most popular comedian of the day, he was selling plenty of bonds that night, too.

Once during the melee, Fairbanks disappeared from the stage. When he finally was missed, Chaplin and Lloyd ran around calling out, "Boy lost! Boy lost!" and generally cutting up. Just when the crowd really was wondering what in the world had happened to Fairbanks, he swung down from a limb of the big pepper tree, as agile as any monkey, and leaped some eight feet to the stage with the greatest of ease. He was noted for his leaps and acrobatics in action movies, and he got a tremendous ovation. When he sold more bonds than Chaplin, he obligingly bent forward, making a table of his back, so that Chaplin could write his thousand-dollar check. After two hours of this, Fairbanks invited everyone to go to the auditorium of a nearby building and see Mary Pickford in person. A fascinated participant, I raced to get a seat on the aisle, near the stage.

When the stage curtains rolled back, the big audience fell silent. Then, as drums rolled, a tiny little figure came from the wings — Mary Pickford in a white ruffled knee-length frock, blue ribbon sash, and a wide picture hat topping her long blond curls. The crowd went into a frenzy. The band struck up "Let Me Call You Sweetheart," and hundreds of voices joined in. It was a moving tribute to this young woman who had come to be "everybody's sweetheart."

I'll never forget my first impression of this dainty woman who looked like a child wearing the long curls that were her trademark, nor the shock I had when at last she was allowed to speak. Instead of the girlish soprano one expected, her contralto voice, almost a bass, said in a broad British accent, "I won't say I am not frightened, for I *ah-am!*" She came to the edge of the stage and began to take the money for war bonds from outstretched hands. Guards soon had to move her back before she was pulled into the orchestra.

Later, it was my privilege to talk to Miss Pickford backstage, again courtesy of Miss Loyola. It was a brief but momentous encounter for me. Also present were Beth Fairbanks (Douglas Fairbanks' wife) and Doug, Jr., then nine years old. Miss Pickford actually seemed shy standing there as if poised for flight. "Texas?" she asked in her deep voice. "I've always wanted to go to Texas. Doug here would like to see the cowboys, but I'd like to see the Alamo." Close up, she was beautiful, although the heavy makeup required for her appearance belied her "little girl" impression. I told her she was the favorite star of all Texas, and she seemed delighted. All too soon, a bodyguard led her away.

I was to have another, surprising contact with this unusual young woman. Several days later, as I was walking along a street in downtown Los Angeles, a small woman in a navy blue suit and a cloche came down the sidewalk stairway of a photographer's studio. When she saw me, she paused briefly and said in her low-pitched voice, "Hello, there! I hear you are going back to Texas. Be happy!" I never knew how she knew that and was astonished that she recognized me, having seen me briefly just one time. No wonder she was admired and loved.

It grieves me, even now, to remember how this caring woman became involved in one of the first sensational and nationally most explosive scandals of the film colony. The romance between Pickford and Fairbanks was carried on for a long time in secret and was not even suspected by their public. Fairbanks chafed under the hush-hush restrictions, Hollywood friends told me afterwards. But Pickford fought any disclosure, fearing the anger of her mother and sister, who ruled her every thought and action, and the threat to her spectacular career.

Finally, Beth Fairbanks published accusations, naming dates and places. Partly because Beth Fairbanks overreacted, partly because of Fairbanks' debonair, so-what attitude, and largely because Pickford's adoring public did not want to recognize that their sweetheart had feet of clay, the clamor subsided. Fairbanks and Pickford were married. Court records revealed that Beth Fairbanks and her young son, Douglas, Jr., were paid a sum far greater than Fairbanks was paid for a picture and that Owen Moore, Mary's husband, was paid $100,000 by Pickford. There was surprisingly little condemnation from the public, and the careers of both stars continued to boom.

In spite of my sincere desire to fit into the writers group of the film colony, I terminated my career abruptly. Suddenly, it did not seem worthwhile. This was due, I think, to a number of things: the wartime hysteria, the disappointment of not having any of my film stories accepted, growing homesickness, the distraction of a promised love and security, home and family by Hal. I decided that fame was a fickle Lorelei; love was real.

I marvel now at my failure to perceive the impact the growing film industry would have on the nation. Although I had a small part in it, I did not realize its significance, largely because of the drastic changes war was bringing and the slow maturing of my mind and character. I think few, if any, of the pioneer film makers themselves realized what they were creating and that films would soon "talk." The first long-distance telephone service had startled the world only two years earlier. The first sound-on-film reels were five years away, and the first all-talking movie would not be made for another ten years. Only the dreamers anticipated the technology that would create a worldwide industry of untold wealth. Whether it was a mistake to leave Hollywood at that time or not, it could certainly be termed a missed opportunity. This reasoning was not in my mind, however, in January of 1918. I returned to Dallas and the Old Mill. It was good to be home. I had no regrets.

I had mixed feelings about seeing Hal again. In our letters and in the last telephone call he had made to me—at Miss O'Connor's home—we felt awkward and spoke with pent-up emotion. When we finally met, it was a noisy reunion cheered on by my roommates. After homemade cake and ice cream and some sprightly songs by two of my apartment mates, we were finally alone on the porch swing.

Hal had six days before he was to ship out with his navy unit. Every evening, he traveled from Fort Worth to see me, and we planned a quick wedding. One evening he said, "Now when you live with my mother. . . ." I was startled. There flashed through my mind familiar scenes at his home, where seven rowdy sons harassed a loving but constantly upset mother.

"Live with your mother? Why, I'm not going to do that! I have a good job here. I'll stay right where I am until you come back!"

With an arrogance I had never seen in him before, he said, "No Lattimore's wife ever worked."

"Then I'll not be a Lattimore's wife!"

He left with his dignity wounded. I cried, but not for long.

11.

The Love of My Life

When I returned to a Dallas teeming with war excitement, I was welcomed by my friends in our apartment in Mother Glenn's home. Living there were Dora George, a former Baylor College classmate recruiting students for the school; Else Thiessen, a charming German girl who taught at the Hockaday School for Girls; and Ruth Glenn, daughter of our landlady, still in college and a talented pianist. We had our pick of dates. Hundreds of young men were filling the war training camps; Camp Bowie at Fort Worth, an army cantonment just thirty miles from Dallas; Love Field in Dallas, a training field for aviation officers; and a Dallas camp for Canadian aviation cadets. War industries also brought professionals and skilled workers from many states to Dallas in a concerted effort to help win the war-to-end-all-wars.

As the war activities boomed, the social life of Dallas boomed with them. Our little group had favorite dates, but often a dozen or more young men would show up for an evening of fun with Ruth at the piano, Else singing arias with her great voice, and with cards and other games of all description. We seldom left the house. Clare O'Conner, a witty Irish cadet, and Sergeant Turner, with his English accent, good tenor voice, and swank mustache, were often the life of the party. (We admired the slim men in their trim uniforms with glamorous insignia.)

News from the war zones was in grim contrast to the merrymaking, which often was a conscious effort to ease the anxiety of the young trainees. The Russian empire was collapsing under the Bolshevik revolution. The Allies, including the United States, were suffering great losses on the European battlefields. Gold stars indicating the loss of a son, husband, or father were appearing in more and more windows. Hundreds of young Americans were dying in camps of influenza, casualties of a nationwide influenza epidemic.

One night in late May when our group at Mother Glenn's had dates with the Canadian cadets, O'Conner called to tell us their leaves were canceled because one cadet laughed at inspection. We decided to wash our long hair and spend the evening in our apartment. When the telephone rang, an unfamiliar masculine voice asked:

"Is this Bess Whitehead?"

"Yes."

"From Brownwood?"

"Yes—who is this?"

"This is Hubert Scott."

"Oh-o!" My roommates' ears pricked up. "I thought you were dead!"

"Well, sometimes we arise from the dead—Lazarus did! I saw your mother in Brownwood the other day. She asked me to call you when I got to Dallas."

"Then why don't you come out to see me?"

"It's late, child." When he last saw me, I was a skinny ten-year-old with bandages on my head.

"If you call me a child, you'd better come to see me," I challenged.

"I'll be there in fifteen minutes."

He was. Dark and handsome, suave and charming, he obviously was surprised to see a rather attractive and very grown-up woman as composed as he was. We sat in the porch swing until a very late hour, comparing our experiences since 1900. While I had continued in school, taught languages, and entered my communications career, he had worked on the Santa Fe Railroad as a "butch," then brakeman, refusing further promotions because they were inside the train —too confining. He had become a traveling salesman and spent several years in South America in sales promotions. He had joined the U.S. Marine Corps in October of 1916. His division was destined to fight one of the bitterest battles in Europe—Belleau Woods. But he was not with them. Instead, in early 1917 when rebels caused trouble in the Dominican Republic, then a U.S. protectorate, sixty-seven mounted U.S. Marines were sent to put down the uprising. Hugh (as he liked to be called) was with them but within months became a war casualty. As he and a fellow Marine were riding down a main street, he was shot by a sniper. Fortunately, a hospital vessel was in port. He was operated on and then sent to the U.S. Marine Hospital in Philadelphia, where he stayed four months. Given a medical discharge in late 1917, he returned to Brownwood and his family, whom he had not seen for twelve years. "They thought I was dead," he said. "You know there was not much in Brownwood to go home to." I thought that a callous remark, and it bothered me; but I let it pass.

As we parted that night in Dallas, he kissed me and suggested I meet him for breakfast the next morning at the Adolphus Hotel. I did. For the next three weeks, I met him for breakfast and dinner each day and was with him until late hours every night. In less than a week, he had begun to tell me that he was tired of wandering. He had found a sales job in Dallas. He wanted to settle down, put down roots, have a family. The second week, he enlarged on this theme and declared it had to be with me. At the end of the third week, on April 27, 1918, we were married by Dr. George Truett in his study at the First Baptist Church.

Although I was quite obviously swept off my feet, I had told Hugh I would not leave the Hulsey Theatres until the war was over, or until the end of the year. Everyone was sure the end of the war was in sight, and it was—the Armistice was signed November 11. So, on December 23, 1918, with my Christmas holiday already earned, I said farewell to my associates at the Old Mill office, and also to Texas. Hugh by then was employed to establish dealerships for King Candy Company of Fort Worth and was given the territory of Missouri, Kansas, and Colorado. He estimated we could cover Missouri in three months, Kansas in another three, and then settle down in Denver.

I was to learn his itching feet would never settle down, that a job would always be secondary to a change of pace or place; that with a hundred dollars in his pocket, Hugh Scott viewed the world through rose-colored glasses and the words "a thought of tomorrow" were not in his vocabulary. As long as there was another hundred dollars out there, he'd find it.

This was a new, exciting existence to me. Hugh crisscrossed Missouri and Kansas by the trains he always loved. I spent the weeks making friends at newspaper offices and going to movies and shows. When Madame Schumann-Heink gave a concert in Kansas City, I sat with friends in the press box. Only our group knew that the great singer had just heard that her oldest son, fighting on the side of the Germans, had gone down with his submarine. She sang superbly as always and, as was her custom, sang requests at the end of the formal program. The audience loved it. Finally, someone asked for "Taps." In the press box we held our breath as we watched her reaction. The audience did not know why she sang the mournful dirge with such feeling and quickly left the stage.

When Hugh returned to me on weekends, we celebrated new honeymoons, ate gourmet dinners. He knew well how to order the meal, with just the right wine to enhance the food. In those days, cigarette-smoking was not known to be detrimental to one's health, but it certainly was considered detrimental to a woman's character. Hugh insisted that I smoke with him. I could not take his strong Home Runs, so he bought me Chesterfields. In a few weeks, Scotch began to replace the wine in Hugh's glass, and bottles in paper sacks began to appear furtively in our hotel in the dry state of Kansas.

In all my life, I had had no real experience with liquor and its effects. It was not allowed in our home as I grew up, and a drunkard was considered a disgrace to the family and the community. At first, I only noticed that a few drinks made for jolly gatherings with friends; but slowly I began to realize that moodiness, sullenness, and ill temper in Hugh often followed the merriment of an evening. That, of course, brought remorse, unspoken for a long time but evident in the little ways of concern and endearment. I tried to hide my worry. I knew there was real love in our marriage. What was wrong? Was it my fault?

St. Patrick's Day of 1919 was a Monday. Hugh had told me the week before that he would be at home Saturday through Monday at our hotel in Topeka. He was proud of his Irish heritage and often spoke of the celebrations his redheaded father and his grandfather had enjoyed as proud Irishmen. On Friday morning, a bellboy came to my door with two dozen green carnations just delivered from a Topeka florist. I smiled to myself as I knew my Irishman had started his celebration early.

That afternoon the bellboy brought two dozen more green carnations and said the florist would "send the rest of the flowers later." I called immediately and canceled any further orders. To no avail. Two dozen more were delivered Saturday morning. Hugh came in around noon, and I saw at once that he had been celebrating for hours. My disillusionment hurt but stiffened my resolve against any further celebration of St. Patrick. I ordered dinner to be brought to our room instead of the steak and wine dinner I had planned in the dining room. I expected arguments, but my Irish lad was too far in his cups to argue. He refused the food, poured his coffee in the wash basin, and poured a stiff drink from the bottle he took from his suitcase. After a weak rebellion when I refused to share his bed, he fell into a sleep that I knew would hold him for hours.

When I was certain he was beyond hearing me, I called the railroad station and learned that a train left at midnight that would put me into Brownwood the next night. I felt like the abused heroine of a dime novel as I packed my suitcase, removed bills from Hugh's wallet, and took a taxi to the station, where I waited for my train. I did not sleep much that night. By the next evening, I was at Jess's ranch near Brownwood "on a visit." Unlike the fictional heroine, I had not left a note in Topeka.

Two days later, Hugh called the ranch from Brownwood. Guessing that I would be too embarrassed to tell my family the true circumstances, he told them that he was taking a little St. Patrick's vacation to come after me. He was debonair and at his charming best— quite sober. He rode the pastures with Jess and charmed the whole family, including my mother. On the train trip back to Kansas he was the perfect lover and husband. The debacle in Topeka was never mentioned.

We reached Denver, Colorado, the third state of our territory, in May in a snowstorm and went to the Brown Hotel. Snow in May? I had not seen snow in years. It was beautiful. Although I missed the Texas spring, I loved Colorado, where both my children would be born.

We soon found an apartment and Hugh introduced me to a boyhood friend, Louis Brown. Louis was a brother to Herman and George Brown of Houston, founders of Brown and Root. Louis and his wife Jean welcomed us to Denver. In June, the four of us spent an unforgettable two-week vacation at Estes Park. In 1919, Estes Park was far from the beautiful resort it is now, consisting then of one modest club house and several log cabins. But it was a magnificent spot of natural beauty. Hugh and Louis enjoyed each other immensely. Jean and I became fast friends. Since Louis did not drink, neither did Hugh. It was an ideal vacation.

Hugh was an innovative and enthusiastic salesman, and he had succeeded well in establishing dealerships for King Candy Company, especially in florist shops, where he arranged unusual window displays of flowers with the colorful candy boxes. The company had complimented his work and was offering him an expanded territory. His salary and commissions brought us a good income, a princely one in my opinion. But permanence in job or place was anathema to Hubert Scott. Soon after we settled in Denver, he left King Candy and took short-term promotions, selling stocks or bonds, his favorite challenge, working for commissions only. He still traveled, but not so much and not so far. He began selling stock in a proposed auto racetrack to be built on the outskirts of Denver. To my relief, there was no heavy drinking.

As Hugh was assembling his sales crew, Louis asked him to consider his younger brother, George. For some reason, George, who then was a student at the prestigious Rice Institute in Houston, had been judged there as persona non grata, Louis said, and was at loose ends. So George joined the Scott crew of salesmen in Denver for a project that failed in a few months. This story has an O. Henry ending: George returned to Houston and forty years later had made a fortune and was a trustee of the school that expelled him.

Soon Hugh was leading another promotion centered in Denver. I was twenty-eight and he was thirty-two. We both wanted children. I knew he would be a proud and loving father and would always make money easily, although he never saved it. In my heart, I knew he would never settle down, and my common sense told me his drinking problem was a serious one. But when you are in love it is easy to accept promises.

So on Halloween, 1920, our little girl was born. "The child that is born on the Sabbath Day is fair and wise and happy and gay,"

Hubert Scott, Denver, Colorado, 1920

quoted the happy father. He wired "Aunt Lila" Danforth in Houston, naming the baby as he did so: "Lila Bess has arrived. Redheaded like her Auntie. Mother fine and Daddy will survive."

The Browns had no children, and both Jean and Louis found new fascination in watching our precocious baby grow into a definite personality. I dared hope Hugh might follow Louis's suggestion to buy a home in Denver. But this dream was shattered when the promising promotion of the racetrack suddenly fell apart, and Hugh told me we would move to Colorado Springs, where he had signed a contract for partnership in a merchandising business. I was never consulted in these business dealings, although before marriage I had made a successful career on my own. This hurt, but at the time my greatest desire was that I be able to give my child a good life and that Hugh's new business associates would not be drinking companions.

Since we lived in a furnished apartment, the move was little trouble, but leaving Jean and Louis was a real wrench. Jean had been the only close friend I had made since leaving Texas. I found Hugh had already been to Colorado Springs, had leased a house, and had

The Scott family, Colorado Springs, 1922

arranged for the grassy backyard to be fenced in for a safe playground. He also had arranged for me to furnish the house completely, the expense to be a part of his partnership agreement.

I took up this task with vim and a determination to do my part to make the new venture a success. Lila Bess proved to be an extremely active child, never sleeping more than thirty minutes during the day and waking many times in the night. She would not stay in her bed. To let Hugh get needed sleep, I would go with her in her bedroom at night. If I attempted to let her cry it out, Hugh would go sleep with her. This did not help a troublesome family situation, and worry and lack of sleep were eroding the good health I had enjoyed for years.

Then, at age thirty-one, I found I was pregnant. A growing and constant pain proved to be caused by an infection from the first childbirth, but the operation I needed could not be done because of the pregnancy. This was an unexpected crisis, and Hugh asked if I'd like to call Mother, who we knew would come immediately. But I was determined not to ask her to share our troubles again. Hugh agreed, and in the next trying months gave me all the love and help that was possible.

We found a caring neighbor would give us selfless help. There was not ready-to-eat baby food in those days. Mrs. Lawson made it her job to sterilize bottles and milk and cook daily the mixtures of meats and vegetables and the fruit blends Lila Bess needed. She also taught the baby to use her bowl and spoon and to drink from her cup. And when our little black-eyed "Scotty" was born, April 29, 1922, and I had reached the point that I could not even lift him, Mrs. Lawson became his beloved protector and nurse. Hugh was home most of the time. He delighted in taking our little blond daughter to the store and for half days to his office, where she was the center of attraction. Lila visited us during her vacation and was astonished at the vocabulary of her precocious namesake. In the only way he knew, Hugh tried to atone for any neglect in the past. He brought me flowers, beautiful records for our Victrola, and lovely clothes, even hats, although I could wear them and go out with him only occasionally.

Finally, when Scotty was seven months old, we decided on the operation that our doctor told us frankly I might not survive. Mother came from Texas to be with me. In another six months, I was almost back to normal and agreed to our next move. Restless for weeks, Hugh had returned to the work he liked best — promotions and selling. I knew that his sights were on California.

In a two-door Model A Ford sedan, we drove from Colorado Springs to Los Angeles over hills and dales and desert draws — the deep, dry gullies that cross that desolate area. Mother had consented to go with us, knowing my need for her. Jim, a young salesman who worked for Hugh, went along. Four adults with two babies, milk and formulas in portable ice chests, and a great supply of diapers (not disposable in those days), we sailed along, often passing big cars. Hugh made a hilarious safari of the trip, hanging wet diapers on the hood like white flags, stopping to let the children play, and taking pictures. Mother proved a surprisingly good sport, and Jim was a real help with his cheerful good humor. We felt like pioneers. I was thankful there was no drinking, not ever beer.

Hugh had arranged with a salesman friend to rent a house for us. Within a week, we were settled in a pleasant neighborhood, and the children were enjoying a big backyard and California sunshine. Within another week, Hugh and Jim were working on a promotion, which failed to get off the ground. Their sales crew left to undertake another project in North Carolina.

The next six months in Los Angeles were a time of recuperation for me. The children played outside and were less care. Mother and I lived quietly and had good neighbors. All of us enjoyed the beach. The days were without stress. Partly in an attempt to compensate for past mistakes, and largely because he was trying to fulfill a dream of settling down, Hugh sent me generous checks and suggested I buy new furniture and move to a house nearer to the beach.

"Pshaw!" said Mother. "He will never settle down. This is foolish."

But it was a new interest, and I was restless and unhappy at the long separation of our family. So I bought good furniture for a three-bedroom, two-bath house, choosing colors and a decor that I knew would please my husband. Hugh and his crew went to Washington State and northern California for another six months.

When Hugh finally came home, after a year with only a Christmas visit to us, he announced that we were all moving to San Diego, where the nucleus of his sales crew was already setting up another promotion that would continue for more than a year. They would sell stock to finance several additions to the pink stucco U.S. Naval Center on San Diego Bay. Hugh had already been there and had rented an attractive house that had a large attic with dormer windows and beautiful landscaped yards. It was on a dead-end street with terraced

Lila Danforth and the author in the woods near San Diego, California, 1922

slopes down to a shallow ravine, "a perfect place for the children to play in safety," my unpredictable Irishman assured me.

Our furniture was moved from Los Angeles, and the ensuing twenty months were another happy period in my married life. Hugh was home with us the entire time, again the exciting playmate and loving father and husband. He did not drink. During the spring and summer, we spread our mattresses on the floor of the half-story attic and enjoyed the sea breezes and the fragrance of a huge running rosebush that shaded our balcony and covered much of the roof. Mother decided to visit my sister in Washington state and then go home to Brownwood. It had become hard for her to accept Hugh's eccentricities and to hide her disapproval of his carefree ways, although he really loved "Mama Whitehead."

"If he goes away again, or starts drinking, you come home," she told me. "You always have a home with your family in Texas." She knew it would take something tragic to make me do that. But I was grateful. Dear Mama. Always on call.

As the work in San Diego drew to an end, Hugh began to talk about going back to Texas. I was dismayed and tried to discourage it. I knew what would happen when he got with his drinking friends there, and I could not face the constant disapproval of my family and the stress on our sensitive little girl. She had gone through a period of being afraid of her father, but this had subsided, and she felt secure again in his love.

But when I realized that Texas it must be, I told Hugh I would never move furniture again, that I wanted to sell everything and that I wanted to visit my sister Elizabeth in Ellensburg, Washington, before I went to Texas. He agreed at once. We had a dealer come out and make an offer, and we sold everything in the house, including the children's tricycles and the yard slides and swings. I put the children in our big Marmon car, picked up a nurse who wanted to exchange her care of the children on the trip for her passage to Seattle, and drove up the coastal highway north. Hugh was to finish up his work and meet me in a month in Houston.

From Seattle, I drove east over the Cascades to Ellensburg. The narrow mountain roads in that day were unpaved and had sharp curves. The speed limit was fifteen miles an hour. To pass, the car on the cliff side of the road had to pull into one of the niches carved into the cliff. Only logs laid on the rim of the road offered any protection against falling down the mountainside. It was a traumatic experience, made more so by a car with two men who refused to pass me when I gave them room and followed me on the last half of the drive. When I finally came to the sloping road, I pushed my big car to its limit. But the car behind passed and stopped me. A highway policeman in uniform walked back to my car. The children were just waking up. Hysterical with relief, I exploded. I didn't even know I knew the names I called him. He heard me out in silence.

"I saw you were alone with little ones in the car. I thought you might need help on that difficult road. It's not far to the next town —stop and get a cup of coffee," he said calmly.

As we drove on, my observant little daughter commented with the lisp she had not outgrown, "That polithman wath a thtupid athth, wathn't he, Mama?" That one picked up words in a hurry.

Mother was visiting Elizabeth and family in Ellensburg. They welcomed us, and we spent four weeks there, enjoying weekend drives with them to mountain and Columbia River resorts. When we left for Texas, Mother went with us, returning to Jess's ranch at Brownwood. Her home was with her children, whichever one needed her most, but her home base was her little apartment on the ranch.

In Houston I found a house to rent and was as settled as we ever were, when Hugh arrived two days later. I met him at the train. He was staggering drunk. After our happy months in San Diego, this was hard to take, but it was an old story. Instead of taking him home, I drove him to the Rice Hotel, put him in bed, and drove home. I had to tell the disappointed children that he missed his train and would be in later. Scotty cried a little but my foxy Lila Bess just shook her head and remembered Mother's great swear word, "pshaw." She said, "Oh, thaw!"

Hugh came to us next day in a taxi, bringing barbecue for a picnic dinner. He rolled on the floor and played bear, then put the delighted and exhausted children to bed. Nothing was said about the previous day. He slept soundly, but the uncertainty of the days ahead kept me tossing most of the night.

Within a few months we were on the go again. The promotion

to build an auto racetrack between Houston and Galveston had failed, leaving shattered friendships and debts. It had been a summer of hard drinking and, for the first time, much of it was done at home. Scotty, too young to understand was hurt and puzzled to find his "bear" playmate turned grouchy and irritable. Lila Bess was again coming to me before greeting her father and asking in a whisper, "Is Daddy drinking?" As usual, Hugh was never idle. He signed with Parker Land Company of La Feria in the Rio Grande Valley, and we moved to a house in that small town. The lemons that grew in our yard were as sweet as the oranges. Hugh's schedule kept him in Chicago nearly two weeks rounding up prospects. He brought them by train each second weekend to La Feria, where I met them in our big car and drove them for three days over the land and orange groves that were for sale. The prospects stayed at the company club house, and Hugh was able to come home to be with us at night. Sunday nights, he returned to Chicago, usually having made good sales.

I tried living in a family hotel in Chicago for a time. But we hated the confinement, no play space, and coal dust. We were on the sixth floor, and I was constantly afraid one of the rambunctious children might fall from the balcony. We soon returned to the little house in La Feria. It was September, 1926.

Lila Bess would be six October 31, so I enrolled her in her first school. Scotty was happy with his collie puppy and his little pedal-operated red car in which he drove to the post office daily. There was always a letter from Daddy. As long as we were married, he rarely failed to write me a brief letter each night, on his hotel stationery, and I have a trunk full of them. Except for a lurking fear that some weekend Hugh would not be on the train, I was reasonably relaxed. And I had good neighbors.

Then on the first weekend of November, Hugh was not on the train. I waited until all the passengers were off. One of the salesmen walked over: "Don't believe Scott brought any prospects this time, Mrs. Scott." I saw embarrassment and compassion in his eyes. He knew I knew.

That whole week no letter came from Hugh. And no check came to me from Parker Land Company, as had been the arrangement.

I used up the little cash I had. Then Mr. Parker asked me to come to his office. I knew in my heart the end had come. When I told him I had not heard from Hugh in over a week, he said, "I'm sorry," and I knew he was. "Scott disappeared from Chicago ten days ago. Does he drink to excess, Mrs. Scott?" He saw the answer in my face.

"Scott was one of our best salesmen, but he always overspent his expense account. We liked him. He has great ability and charm. You understand the company cannot continue sending you a check. But if you need funds at the moment, I'll see that you get them."

I thanked him, assured him I did not need help, knowing that I had hamburger meat, bread, and milk—and less than a dollar in cash.

I knew my brothers would help—I had only to call upon them. But pride and the instinct to protect Hugh from criticism held me back. I turned as I always had to Lila in Houston.

"Come at once," she told me when I called. "Do you need me to send you money?"

I told her I did not. I went to the local bank and borrowed a hundred dollars on my engagement ring, picked up Lila Bess at school, and spent the rest of the day having the car serviced and packing our belongings. Scotty agreed to give his beloved toy auto to a little neighbor boy when I told him he could take his puppy to Houston. So the next morning, with a steamer trunk, suitcases, a collie puppy, and two excited children, we left for Houston.

The love and concern of my loyal friends, Lila and Dad Danforth, were balm to my wounded heart. Lila had cleared a big storeroom for Scotty and me and shared her room with Lila Bess. Within a week, we had Lila Bess in school and I had part-time work at the *Houston Press*. Dad had his print shop in his side yard and looked after Scotty until I could get him into kindergarten. Not only was the big Marmon not paid for but I could not afford to run it, and we had good bus transportation. I wrote the San Diego dealer, and his representative picked up the car. Scotty cried, and so did I silently, but for a different reason. To me, it was the beginning of the end of a beautiful exhilarating, trusting dream. I was humiliated, disillusioned, and sad. I prayed I would not let the hurt become bitterness, and I prayed for the strength to shield my children from such hurt as long as I could. I still had hope—hope that "love *could* conquer all." Hugh was the love of my life.

Within four weeks, Scotty and I were living in "housekeeping rooms" in an old home next to the *Houston Press*. Lila Bess had chosen to stay with Aunt Lila and her collies and Persian cats. I put Scotty in kindergarten only two blocks from the *Press* plant, and at noon he came to me in the city room and played quietly until my day was over at three. I often took him with me on assignments.

Three months after leaving us, Hugh wrote me from Oklahoma City, enclosing a money order that was three times my weekly salary. He wrote in care of Lila and wanted to come back to us. When he arrived, I think our drab little apartment and our separation from Lila Bess brought home to him more than anything else the guilt of his desertion. With a contriteness and remorse that were sincere, he vowed to have us all together in a nice home within days. He went to work immediately as a salesman for an old and reliable bonding firm, and his first week's commission was quadruple my salary. But I refused to give up my job or even to move, and declared him "on probation" for a month. He agreed to the terms and did not drink at all.

Then late one Friday after Lila had picked Scotty up for the weekend, Hugh came home "on top of the mountain." He was not drinking, but filled with his old enthusiasm. He had found the greatest opportunity of his life. It was the work that was made for him, and he for it. I would love it!

I could not speak. All the old fears crowded in on me. He did not take notice of my silence.

"I've been in Galveston all day," he spoke without pause, "talking to the Nehi Company, makers of Orange Crush—you know that popular orange drink that everybody loves. I've signed a contract to establish dealerships all over the Southern states. I'll have you and the children with me in two weeks. We've got to get Lila Bess back —we'll have a home again, little Mother!"

"Where?" I managed to ask.

"In New Orleans! I have to leave on the seven o'clock train—get ready, honey, and go to the station with me—we just have an hour!"

For the first time in the many months since we had left San Diego, moving to Washington, Houston, the Valley, Chicago, and Houston again, I completely broke down. I was hysterical and could not stop crying. Dismayed, Hugh tried to console me, picturing a life together "like it was in San Diego." He had learned his lesson, he said. He loved me and our babies above everything else in the world. He could not go on without us. And he would never, never drink again. That promise, sincerely meant at the moment, but which I knew to be hollow, stiffened my will. I did not argue. I was convinced New Orleans, one of Hugh's favorite cities, filled with friends who "lived by the bottle" would end all hope for us. I went to the station with him, and he paid the cab to wait to take me home. He took my arm and led me across the many tracks to the end of the train, still talking of our great future. As the cars began to move, he kissed me and, as always, swung up to the end platform. As the train rounded the curve out of sight, he was still waving good-bye to me.

I never saw him again. Seven months later, on our tenth wedding anniversary when I went to work at the *Press* at 7:30 A.M., I found a telegram from Minneapolis on my typewriter, with no return address: "Anniversary Greetings. Will always love you—Hugh."

12.

Back Home to the *Houston Post*

In 1927, another chapter in my life began. My marriage was over, Lila had given us refuge while I returned to my profession. It was not easy. I had not worked as a journalist in nine years. The tempo of the times had speeded up, and the economy was slowing down. World War I had disrupted the old, deliberate pattern of living. The struggle to cope was getting harder. But I had a greater incentive now than just ambition. I had two children to care for.

When I applied for work at the *Post,* Charlie Maes, now general manager, remembered me well. He could not place me on his staff, but he sent me to see Ellen MacCorquodale at the *Houston Press,* a Scripps-Howard afternoon daily. An influential member of the Houston media scene, and formerly with the *Post,* she now was amusements and arts editor of the *Press.* When I told her of my experience in writing publicity for moving pictures, her eyes sparkled.

"Here," she pushed toward me a Hollywood publicity sheet such as I had written years before. "Take this and write me a preview of this picture."

I quickly finished the story, and when she read it she grabbed my arm. "Come with me," she exclaimed. "You are an angel from heaven!"

"I've found a jewel," she told Managing Editor Webb Artz when she took me to his desk. "You know I hate to write this stuff. Mrs. Scott is a natural; I've got to have her help."

I learned that Miss Mac really did despise the movies and writing about them. Her love was the music and art run. Mr. Artz hired me, three days a week at first, but soon put me on full-time. My salary was below average, only fifteen and then twenty-five dollars a week, but I was thankful to get a start again.

I gave all the ability and energy I had to make the *Press* movies, *talking* movies now, and theater run interesting. Soon I was interviewing show-world personalities.

The Arthur Casey Players were one of the better stock companies of these years. Houstonians were delighted to learn that the leading man for the 1928 season would be a rising and popular young screen player, Clark Gable. Gable was in his twenties, a six-footer, young, awkward, not a little spoiled by his successes, and ripe for the adulation Houston's public would give him. He was welcomed by the city's fast-paced social set.

The Players opened a new play each Sunday night for a week's run. They had to rehearse the following week's play during the day. Gable put his Houston playmates first, cut rehearsals, and often did not know his lines on opening night. His ad libbing infuriated his leading lady, Nancy Duncan, who was older than Gable and a serious, experienced actress. The editors of the *Press,* the *Chronicle,* and the *Post* were aware of the situation and viewed it with some amusement and little sympathy for Gable.

One Sunday night, he seemed to me more than usually careless with his lines and awkward in his scenes with the diminutive Miss Duncan. In my review of the play, I wrote that he made love like a bull in a china shop.

Soon after the first edition of the *Press* hit the streets the next afternoon, Gable appeared at the *Press* office and walked to my desk in the corner of the big city room.

"Mrs. Scott?" He bowed from the waist as I looked at him over my typewriter.

"Yes." I had recognized him and waited.

"I am Clark Gable." He paused for that to soak in. I nodded.

"So I do not know how to make love," he smiled ingratiatingly. "Would you like to teach me?"

"Touché!" I laughed. "Let's go over to the Quick and Dirty and have a cup of coffee. We'll talk it over."

It was the beginning of a long and warm friendship. He played in Houston for two seasons, his popularity and skill increasing. He married Ria Langford, an attractive young widow of Houston who had a small daughter. Although this marriage ended in divorce, Gable came back to Houston years later to give his stepdaughter in marriage. "Hello, little sweetheart," he called to me as I stood with a group of reporters at the airport. It pleased me that he had achieved real fame in his profession, and I grieved at his untimely death a few months before his only child, a son, was born.

When important news events broke, many members of the *Press* staff were assigned to them, regardless of their daily runs. Thus, I was one of several reporters who covered the 1928 Democratic Convention in Houston when Franklin Delano Roosevelt nominated Al Smith of New York for president of the United States. The city room was agog with excitement, and each reporter hoped for a good assignment. Miss Mac had no interest in this event, but I wanted very much to have a part. Several days before the convention opened, with internationally known figures already filling the hotels, Managing Editor Artz loped, as was his fashion, to our corner.

"Do you girls want to help cover the convention?"

Miss Mac looked at me and easily read my mind. "Bess does," she said. "Take her. I'll cover her run for the week."

"All right, Bess. You just circulate around and pick up what interviews and features you can. The shorter the better, but go for the big ones. Try to have your copy in for the first edition." That meant by 10:30 A.M. at the latest. The *Press* was an afternoon paper.

Artz loped back to his desk. No other word describes the way he made his continuous rounds of the city room. Only one other man I have known moved in the same way—my friend Lyndon Johnson.

Unmindful of the summer heat, I joined the army of reporters virtually living at the temporary coliseum the city had built to house the huge convention. I attacked my assignment with zest and felt as though I walked in glory amidst peers, forgetting my personal problems and often distressing my dear mother, who by then was taking care of my children and my home, by returning in the early morning hours and never getting more than four hours of sleep before rushing back to work.

I was heartily commended for one interview, sarcastically flattened by "Mefo," M. E. Foster, autocratic *Press* editor, for another.

To my credit was a near-interview with Roosevelt as I talked to his son James. I had ventured back stage in the coliseum as Roosevelt stood in the wings on his crutches, supported by his son. Here was my chance, but James stood guard.

"I am a reporter. Would you let me speak to your father?"

"I'm afraid not," James said. "You see, he is ready to go on stage."

"Just a word," I pleaded.

Roosevelt looked around his son's shoulder and grinned at me. "Good luck, honey."

"That's the 'word,'" James smiled as they walked on stage to nominate Al Smith, the "Happy Warrior," for president of the United States.

Not much, but good for a boxed story on page one and a "well done" by Mefo.

But, as my mother would say, "pride goeth before a fall." I made my best-remembered faux pas a bit later. I had stopped by the public library on the way to the coliseum and a friendly librarian told me, "You want a story? That is Will Durant, the author, sitting at that table."

Durant's *The Story of Philosophy* had already put him on the road to the place he now holds in the world of letters. I introduced myself. He put aside the book he was reading and in a friendly thirty-minute session discussed his writing and went into a detailed explanation of some of his professional and political views. He candidly predicted that although Al Smith was a fine man and a capable administrator and politician, "being Catholic, he has a slim chance of being elected president—not a good reason but a reason, a victim of religious prejudice."

I rushed back to the *Press* and turned in my copy. Mr. Artz said, "Good work, Bess. Bring me a picture of Durant from the morgue" (a term for a newspaper's library).

I could not find a picture but found a one-column sized "mat," a matrix from which can be cast a metal "cut" for printing. Since it was near deadline for the first edition of that day, Mr. Artz hurriedly marked directions on the copy for the press room as I wrote a cutline to be printed under the picture. As soon as the early edition copy reached the city room and Editor Foster, whose office was in a penthouse on top of the *Press* building, Mr. Artz called me to his desk. Silently he pointed to Mefo's written words on the margin of the Durant picture, "This is NOT Will Durant." We had used a picture of Will Durant, manufacturer of the Durant automobile then in wide use. Mr. Artz was kind enough to take the blame. A likeness imprinted on matrix paper is hard to recognize. "We were in too big a hurry," was his only comment.

Several times while I was on the *Press* staff, Mr. Artz asked me to do research on important stories top reporters were covering, a case of a woman doing the work but the man taking the credit. I resented this to some extent, but in time I realized it was of real benefit to me in acquiring knowledge as well as experience. I am grateful for the association with such "pros" as Webb Artz; Dudley Davis, who was to die tragically in an auto accident; Andy Anderson, a great sportswriter; George Carmack, a later editor; and Carmack's future wife, Bonnie Jo, who trained as a cub in our department. And of course, Miss Mac.

Ellen MacCorquodale was a tall, broad-shouldered woman with a masculine stride; her beauty of face was enhanced by a vibrant charm, which made her quite attractive when she chose to exert it. Miss Mac was a rare spirit, a woman with a great ability to instill in her coworkers her intense regard for integrity in reporting. She was a punishing mixture of sensitive emotion and harsh judgments, of herself as well as others. She had a fierce pride in her work that at times blurred her perspective and caused her unjustified anguish. It also made her overly jealous of what she considered her prerogatives, so that she often antagonized her fellow workers, although she was a compassionate friend to those she trusted. Men on the staff feared her caustic tongue; women sought to avoid her unpredictable changes of mood.

Later, I came to better understand that disloyalties, rejections, disillusionment, and what she considered betrayal in her personal life accounted in part for her occasional abrasive words and acts.

Under Miss Mac, I was to learn true self-discipline and a deep and lasting regard for accuracy and truth in reporting. Through her, I made many unforgettable friends: Mrs. Edna Saunders, a concert manager who brought top-flight musical and drama artists to Houston, and her aide, Mrs. Perkins, who never wore anything but severely tailored men's suits and yet was a genuinely feminine "Southern lady." Mrs. Saunders managed to work smoothly with the art and amusement editors of all three Houston newspapers and held their goodwill, but I felt she sometimes gave Miss Mac, her close friend, tips that the ingenious reporter turned into valued scoops.

I remember one morning when Miss Mac asked me to come to work at seven instead of my usual eight to cover her absence from her desk. I did not ask for an explanation but was at work at the early hour. Near the early edition deadline she rushed in and made her old typewriter talk as she beat out an interview with the great opera tenor, John McCormack. She had met him at the train and interviewed him as they walked to the Rice Hotel. Thus, she scooped the *Post* and the *Chronicle* writers who had to wait until the 2:00 P.M. interview arranged by Mrs. Saunders.

I remember also her grief and humiliation when her interview appeared in the *Press* cut in half by many deletions. She considered the mangled story unworthy of her byline and of Mr. McCormack. Of course, this is an occupational hazard for any reporter whose stories must pass under the blue pencils of editors whose job it is to know the available space in each edition and allot that space as their judgment dictates. I've suffered a broken heart (ego?) many a time when my brainchild has been slashed and not always, in my opinion, with compassion!

Within a year after I began at the *Press,* it was evident to all of us that Miss Mac's health was failing. Close friends knew she was suffering from tuberculosis. Her nervous energy gradually ebbed. Her eyes began to brighten with fever. She came late to work more often, and as the days passed she began to have me do her "legwork" and take my notes to her at home. There she wrote the stories, stamping them with her personality, bent to her style, interpreted with her facile grace. In the office I covered for her in every possible way, but Mr. Artz and a few others knew the situation.

She found it harder to work day by day, but her indomitable will carried her on. When too ill to write, she would send me to get the story or interview and write it. But she required that I take the copy to her at home for her to read before it was turned in to the managing editor. Since my only transportation was the city bus, there were times when the paper deadlines did not allow me to get the copy to her for review, and I would have to turn it in without her seeing it. Gradually, I sensed she was viewing me as a usurper, out to get her job. As I felt this, I was torn between anger and pity.

On two occasions about this time, she astonished everybody when she suddenly showed up in the city room, nervously buoyant. She made no attempt to write and left as suddenly as she came. It was an unhappy time for both of us. I knew Mr. Foster had given orders she was to remain on the staff until she herself decided to leave. Mr. Artz knew I was working under a handicap, and he assigned some of the legwork to others at times. But I wanted to do it as long as I could.

When I went to Miss Mac's home, she asked me to sit in a chair near the door. I knew she was thinking of contagion, but since we handled the same copy, I did not see any point in that. Mrs. Saunders and other friends had urged her repeatedly to go to a hospital for treatments that they felt would cure her. She refused, reportedly for religious reasons.

She called me one day in late afternoon and asked me to come to her house. "No job for you, just come." I went at once.

"Do you remember Charlie Maes?"

"Of course." He had been city editor on the *Post* during my cub days. Miss Mac paused a minute and gazed out the window by her bed.

"He remembers you," she said. "In fact, he has been watching your bylines in the *Press*. The *Post* amusement editor is leaving. Maes is offering you the job."

I was silent, surprised and uncertain. "You would be head of the department with a free rein. The pay is much better, too."

Was she thinking of my future as it seemed — or was she trying to remove a threat to her? She certainly would never be able to return to her *Press* job. And how did she know the *Post* job was open? Questions rushed through my mind. I felt ashamed of them, but I knew I was not mistaken about her jealousy.

"Miss Mac," I said slowly. "I'm afraid it will be some time before you will be well enough to go back to work. I would not want to desert you."

"Nonsense," she replied quickly. "I may never go back, but the *Press* will survive. Go see Charlie tomorrow." Her face was flushed, her eyes too bright, but she smiled as she waved me out. I fought back the tears as I left her, but I knew I would see Mr. Maes.

I never knew exactly why Miss Mac maneuvered to have me leave the *Press*. Knowing the many quirks of her nature, I think it could be a combination of things: wanting to give me security; knowing that the Scripps-Howard *Press*, a chain, had a fast turnover in personnel and favored young reporters; knowing that background politics of the Houston media that I did not know (the *Press* folded some years later); or a fierce pride that made her think she would like to see her "run" split up and deteriorate if she had to give it up. That is what happened later when Hubert Roussel, a superb writer, took on the job and made it one of great worth and appeal. I like to think that Miss Mac was only looking out for my welfare.

At times in her relationship with me, her great heart and inner beauty came through in full measure and healed the hurts and sealed the affection I still hold for her. I often wish I could have known the young Ellen. She must have been a lovable and lovely girl. As I often did in those days when deeply moved, I wrote a verse to my friend:

To Ellen

I never see rose asters now
   Without a thought of you.
Crisp, bristling leaves that gleam in self defense,
Yet yield to tender touch, the seeming prick
   Disarmed by friendliness.

Rose asters have a winter tang
   And lift their heads in pride;
Their frosted beauty hides a golden heart
And guards with jealous zeal a glowing warmth
   Within their chaliced depths.

As asters fade they do not droop
   But dim and sear erect,
High courage holds the shafts aloft
Reluctant to admit a higher will
   And loathe to bow to death.

I never see rose asters now
   Without a thought of you.

After I went to the *Post*, I kept in touch with Miss Mac, visiting her occasionally at her home. She knew she was in the last stages of tuberculosis and so gave up the little home she was buying and moved by ambulance to an apartment. Her faithful housekeeper and friend, Eula, never left her. In the early morning hours of a September day in 1930, as Kathleen Houston, a loyal friend, soothed Miss Mac's death-burning lips with ice cubes, her brave fight ended. She had found solace in the presence of a practitioner from her church who sat across the room reading in a low monotone.

My second career at the *Houston Post* was marked by achievements and failure, joys and sorrows, and intertwined relationships with coworkers, family, friends, and strangers. Time, defined by a writer friend of mine as "that loom upon which the threads of life are woven," had brought many changes—changes in location of the *Post* from downtown to a suburban location, healthy growth and changes in ownership and staff (and a name change, *Post-Dispatch,* until the paper was sold again), phenomenal growth in the city of Houston, and changes in me through experience and maturity. My friend Lila, now secretary to Congressman Dan Garrett, had taken my nine-year-old Lila Bess with her to Washington, D.C. My eight-year-old Scotty was "Street and Bridge Commissioner" of his Eastwood Elementary School. My loyal mother continued to keep a home for me and my son. She made it possible for me to do night assignments for a morning paper with no worries about my little family.

As I sat down at the desk assigned me by City Editor Max Jacobs ("Jake" to everybody) that February day in 1929, I felt I was home again. It seemed to me I had lived a lifetime in the fourteen years that had passed since I had made a deal with Harry Warner to enter newspaper work. I did not look back. I was unaware of the coming of the Great Depression, and the challenge of a new career made the future look bright to me.

The next fifteen years probably were the busiest of my life. I had returned to the *Post* as amusement editor, which in those days included the theater, movie, art, and music runs. But my assignments eventually would include features, interviews, school news, including meetings of a controversial school board, Rotary Club meetings, church news, promotional stories, conventions, and working with teams of reporters to cover exceptional news events in a rapidly growing city.

Lila Bess Scott and Lila Danforth in Washington, D.C., 1929

Unlike 1915 when I was the only woman reporter on the city side, now there were two others in the *Post* city room, Pat McNealy and Melba Newton. They were young and exceptionally capable reporters.

We three were accorded equal status with men in similar work — with one exception: we were never paid equal salaries for equal work. I regret to say in many cases this inequality still exists. My salary at the *Post* at that time was $30.00 a week. In the fifteen years I was there, the salary was never more than $37.50, and, during the depression years, it was cut to $27.50. Like everyone else who could, I moonlighted.

But on that Monday morning in 1929 when I started my job as amusement editor, I was satisfied with the salary. It was more than the twenty-five dollars I had been paid at the *Press* and average for a woman (and the dollar was then worth many times what it is now). My rent for a four-room apartment was thirty dollars per month. Our family of three lived comfortably on a salary that also had to cover bus transportation and lunches for me. I have always been humbly grateful that all during the depression and two world wars, I was never without a job. My mother had her own income for her few needs, and although I did not allow her to bear any of our living expenses she spent her money generously on the children as it pleased her.

As amusement editor of the *Post* I interviewed many celebrities who gave concerts, road show performances, opera programs, and vaudeville shows in Houston. My recollection of these happenings is largely from memory or undated notes, so they do not follow here in strict chronological order. Few of my contemporaries are living now, and written records are hard to find. All of the personal experiences are clearly in my mind, but exact dates cannot be vouched for, and names of a few minor characters have not been remembered. But all of the following events occurred within the period from 1929 to 1945. It never occurred to me to keep a scrapbook during those busy days. Such a record would have been helpful if I had envisioned myself writing a book about my experiences.

I was not well versed in music, but I found Edna Saunders a valuable friend. She coached me, gave me copies of musical publications, explained technical terms, and in many ways helped me increase my knowledge and vocabulary. Of course, she supplied all of the papers with advance "tear sheets" and publicity stories about the stars and performers.

One nationally popular opera star she brought to Houston was Beniamino Gigli, a contemporary of John McCormack. A well-known Italian businessman in Houston arranged a small wine and spaghetti dinner for Gigli after his concert. I was invited as the host's neighbor, not as a reporter. I was late getting to the party. Everyone was in a lively mood. The effusive Gigli greeted me with a kiss on each cheek and presented me with a lovely little triangular-shaped ivory basket embossed with pink rosebuds that was made in Italy. I was the envy of the other women guests, I knew. It was an evening of ready repartee and much amateur singing led by the irrepressible Gigli. I was glad that my review of his concert, even then rolling through the *Post* presses, was warm and appreciative.

Mr. Maes, at that time the general manager of all *Post* departments, had told me my reviews of movies and other amusement would not be censored. I had decided opinions about these offerings that the public paid for, so I expressed them. I felt a review written for the public should be fair but not restrained by the theater management. I believed the reviewer had a responsibility to the public. A lousy picture or performance should be so described. A worthy offering should be praised. The reaction of an audience should be noted also, I felt. So I tried to write frank, but truthful and fair, reports.

I knew my department was popular reading because of the many approving letters I received. Only a few letters disapproved of my reviews, and some of these, I learned, were inspired by exhibitors. When the letters grew to a sizable number, I suggested to City Editor Max Jacobs that a movie column might be interesting to readers. With Mr. Maes's approval, I started a "Tipping You Off" column that ran five days a week. The source of the tips were movie trade magazines, publicity sheets from film companies, and letters from the public. Almost without exception, the readers' responses were favorable.

But a few local exhibitors objected to my frank reviews of their pictures, notably one personable young man, Homer McCallon of Loew's State Theatre. We argued a lot but viewed each other with mutual respect, even affection. Over coffee cups at the Greasy Spoon we had many a foe-and-friend argument. He argued vehemently that a reporter should *report* only: name of picture, schedule shown, a hint of plot, classification (comedy or drama), and names of stars. I argued that a reviewer owed the public who paid for the entertainment a report on the audience reactions and reviewers' personal opinions.

Much to my surprise, after several months, McCallon went to Mr.

Maes with his complaints. He won. Other theaters advertising in the *Post* joined McCallon in his protest. In a diplomatic manner, I was fired from the movie run. It was transferred from the editorial department of the paper to the advertising department. Money topped art. Reviews continued to be printed, but they were written by the ad salesmen from handouts by the exhibitors!

My head was bloody but not bowed. "Tipping You Off" continued to run and bring in interesting letters from readers. I still reviewed all stage and vaudeville attractions and interviewed the popular stars.

13.

Show People

Show people are among the most loyal friends a person can have if they are truly friends. They are temperamental and often sentimental, egotistical and sensitive, explosive and tenacious, talented, easily hurt, but generous and giving. Most of those who achieve success in their fields have worked tirelessly for it and are worthy of it. Of course, there are, as in all trades, some rotten apples. My happy memories now are of the lovable ones; the others do not matter. In the early and mid-thirties, I made friends to remember.

For instance, there was Katherine Cornell, lovely in person and personality. She played on the Majestic Theatre stage in *The Barretts of Wimpole Street,* and was an appealing Elizabeth Browning. When I called to ask for an interview, she invited me to go to her suite in the Rice Hotel an hour before she was to leave for the evening performance. I was there at the appointed time. She was not. I walked to the window at the end of the corridor and waited. In about thirty minutes she appeared, breathless, with her companion and two small dogs in tow.

"Oh, my dear, I am so sorry," she apologized. "We thought we had plenty of time to take Flush (the little dog in the play) and his little stand-in for a walk to the bayou [she said "bay-oo"]. We had a hard time getting them back—the poor little things are cooped up so much. Then, you know the hotel management makes us use the freight elevators because of the little dogs, and there was just too much freight! We waited and waited and waited! Now we have to get our things together, take that miserable elevator again, and walk to the theater.

"This is what we'll have to do," she said, hardly taking a breath as they gathered their things, guided the dogs on leashes, and were out in the hall again. "You walk to the theater with us, we'll talk as we go, then you talk to me in the dressing room while I put on makeup.

"What an ugly way to treat you—you are so patient!"

I assured her that I'd be delighted to walk up Main Street with her to the theater. We did just that. Miss Cornell asked me as many questions as I did her, seeming genuinely interested in Houston, Texas, Galveston, and me personally. She spoke of how much she loved her role in her play, how she admired the Brownings and their poetry.

"I feel so lucky and so humble to be able to play Elizabeth Browning, a truly inspiring lady," she continued. "I understand there is a wonderful Browning library near here. Do you know of it?"

When I told her the library was some two hundred miles away at Baylor University and I was a graduate of Baylor, she stopped putting on her makeup and exclaimed. "How wonderful! How long would it take to go there? Oh, impossible. I'll have to be in Dallas tomorrow and Denver the next day. I thought the Browning library was near Houston." She was genuinely disappointed. I asked about Flush, the little dog who had a major role in the play. Quickly she told me of her great luck in finding the easily trained little dog, how they always carried two stand-ins for him, and her appreciation of her companion Viola. "She keeps me and the dogs in the best of shape and on our toes, I can tell you. She's a hard taskmaster."

It was nearing curtain time. With renewed apologies, she opened the dressing room door for me. I went out front to enjoy a very special evening, admiring a very gracious lady and a superb actress.

What kind of a review do you think I wrote? Even if she had played like a rank amateur, I think I would have had to hold my barbs.

Another unforgettable star who played at the Majestic was Richard Berry Harrison. He was the first black man ever to occupy the star dressing room there. He played De Lawd in Marc Connelly's *Green Pastures.* He was a handsome man, an actor of dignity and poise. He appeared by nature to fit the role of De Lawd, a benign father and stern taskmaster when dealing with his angel "chillun." He spoke quietly. He liked his role in the play.

I learned this was his first stage role, first lead in a major production. Harrison was then sixty-five years old. He was born in Canada and had been an "elocutionist," reading Shakespearean plays and poems in segregated schools, and a teacher. Connelly described him as having a face "maturely serene," the "inner strength of a gentle being" and having a voice "like a cello." He was a tremendous success as the benign, demanding, but loving, "Lawd."

As I was leaving, noticing his features, I said on impulse, "Mr. Harrison, you do not have the facial characteristics of your race."

He smiled as he delivered his mild rebuke to me.

"What race?"

Just as the depression of the 1930s was slowing down a little, Eleanor Roosevelt, First Lady of the nation for more than twelve years, came through Houston. She was on a speaking tour promoting President Franklin Roosevelt's New Deal, and her special concern was for the youth of the nation and the establishment of work training centers for them.

An interview with her was set for the three Houston papers, and I was sent from the *Post*. When we gathered in her suite at the Rice Hotel, we found young reporters from all the city high schools. All of us were standing in the small room when Mrs. Roosevelt arrived, greeting us with a wide smile.

"What a welcome!" she exclaimed. "Now, I'll take this big chair in the corner as my throne, and all of you children sit on the floor circling me. We will let the newspaper reporters have the other chairs." For the next forty minutes, she told us about her "Crusade for Youth" and answered questions, paying special attention to the students, embracing us with her charm. Her homely features and her voice pitched a bit too high were forgotten. She was a vibrant personality, a friendly, caring neighbor who won us all by her sincere dedication to her crusade to help put America to work again. She took the names of each of the students and later sent each of them a card from the White House.

It was my good fortune to meet this great lady again a year later and ride with her to an afternoon on the Galveston beach. This visit resulted in another more personal interview for my *Post* amusement column. I never considered her homely again.

Less enjoyable were contacts with other top entertainers. Eddie Cantor and Florence Reed, for instance, were openly arrogant and appeared to think they were doing the boondocks a favor to appear on the road. Not only the reporters but the audiences seemed to sense this attitude.

Cantor was a prime favorite in the musical comedy world and was in his late thirties when he brought a skeleton company of singers and dancers to appear with him at the Houston City Auditorium. It was a one-night stand. A group interview with Cantor was set up in his Rice Hotel suite with reporters from the three papers. He kept us waiting for more than thirty minutes, ending all chance for the afternoon papers to print the story that day. Finally, he came out of his bedroom enveloped in a long black dressing robe and stood as expressionless as a store-window model.

After a few attempts at a friendly question session where he mumbled one-word replies when he answered at all, we left. I tried never to wield a vindictive pen at any time, and I have always believed that a public figure has the right to refuse an interview. So I ignored Cantor's rudeness, wrote a review of his show, and did not mention the interview. The *Press* amusement editor, Hubert Roussel, wielded his pen like a dagger after the interview. I will say that I did not fail to write the truth about the show. Cantor was great, but except for one comely young singer with a fair voice, the show suffered in comparison to a small high-school "exhibition."

Florence Reed, an exotic redhead who played in a road show, refused interviews and made enemies of the Majestic Theatre and Rice Hotel staffs by her arrogant demands for privacy and service. Publicity man Bob Kelly said it succinctly: "She's a bad egg." As my dear mother-in-law, always excusing, used to say, "Maybe she had a good mother."

Road shows played often at the Majestic, but between times the theater offered a week's program of newsreels and five acts of vaudeville. One of the acts, usually a stage or movie star, got star billing.

Such a one was Charles Ray, who was remembered from a great screenplay, *The Coward,* in which he played the title role. The story was of Civil War days. Ray played the son of a professional, inflexible Confederate general, who, even in the face of his father's threat to kill him, refused to go to war. Frank Kennan, a longtime screen favorite, played the father in the picture, but another actor played with Ray in the vaudeville act, which was a well-done dramatic scene from the play.

Ray, too, high-hatted the local reporters, much to the dismay of public-relations man Kelly. All papers took a shot at his attitude, although praising his performance. But before the week was half out, he was talking to us—because he had a bee in his bonnet.

"I predict," said Ray with conviction, "that within five years or less we will have small screens within our homes on which to view moving pictures."

Television! None of us talking to Ray that day had even heard the word, although television was being developed in laboratories. Within two years, patents were being issued for certain experiments leading to the process. In 1941, the first commercial broadcast was made from the Empire State Building in New York.

Before his week in Houston was up, Ray told me why he was on a one-act vaudeville tour instead of continuing a successful film career: "You know the old saying about putting all your eggs in one basket, don't you? I'm looking ahead." He wanted diversified training, for when his vaudeville tour was over he intended to try directing and then producing in Hollywood. This was in 1935. In 1943, two years after commercial television was a reality, he died at age fifty-two.

I recall with pleasure a friendship formed at this time with Hobart and Cecile Bosworth, who were pen pals until his death thirteen years later. Bosworth, at that time a distinguished man in his late sixties, had been a stage star for years and at this time was a well-known character actor in films. His was the top act for a week at the Majestic. He came on stage dressed in jodhpurs, carrying a quirt and leading a handsome bay mare—a gentleman ready for the hunt.

It was a sensational entrance that brought instant and hearty applause. His act was made up of a monologue on fox-hunting, moviemaking, and jokes, interspersed with an amusing one-sided conversation with his horse. The mare nodded her head in solemn agreement. One of Bosworth's comments stands out in my memory: "I deplore the vulgarity that is creeping into our moving pictures. We are beginning to indulge in bathroom humor, offensive to most of the public." Loud applause greeted his words.

Bosworth took the amusement editors of Houston's three papers to an elaborate dinner at the Rice Hotel. He was a delightful host. Cecile and I met twice for salad lunches, and she accompanied me and a photographer on an assignment to historical Brazoria County. We exchanged notes and Christmas cards until Bosworth's death in 1943.

A tragic figure at the Majestic in the early thirties was Lou Tellegen, better known for stage roles than for pictures. He was about fifty years old, and his successes were in his past years. His Majestic act consisted of his reciting famous dramatic excerpts from Shakespeare's plays, and while on stage he held his audiences enthralled.

Publicity man Bob Kelly had alerted reporters. "Tellegen is drunk every hour of the day and evening," he told us. "He's really a great tragedian, and you will not detect his drinking while he is on stage. But he may be difficult to interview." I decided to try, so the appointment was made. When I entered the dressing room, Tellegen was slumped in an easy chair. He did not rise but pointed a long finger at me and orated in his best stage manner.

"So you are from the newspaper. Well, let me tell you, newspapers can't *make* me and they can't *break* me!"

I laughed at him and tried to turn the conversation to his fame as a Shakespearean actor. It did not work. He sulked and would not talk. Bob, who had waited in the corridor, finally came to the door and called me. As I left, I called good-bye to Tellegen. He did not look at me, but his voice trailed off.

"The newspapers can't *make* me and they . . ."

"That's the way he stays between shows," said Bob, "just nursing his bottle. I don't know how in hell he can go on stage four times a day and give a great performance."

Lou Tellegen was among the most prestigious Shakespearean actors in his younger years. He married the noted opera singer Geraldine Farrar in 1916; they were divorced in 1920. When he was in Houston, he definitely was on the skids. In 1934 at the age of fifty-eight he stabbed himself to death, one biographer says with "a pair of rusty scissors."

At this apex of my VIP interviewing days there were many enjoyable assignments, but there were dismaying ones, too. One of these was my experience with Madame Schumann-Heink, the beloved opera star.

She called me a liar, addressing her matinee audience from the stage of the Metropolitan Theatre. Since my byline was on the interview story that was printed at the bottom of page one of that morning's *Post,* with a two-column headline, there was no doubt as to whom she was referring when she said the reporter misquoted her.

My first contact with the motherly German singer was not a personal one, but, as mentioned earlier, as a member of an audience in Kansas City, Missouri, in early 1919, when she had sung "Taps" for her son who, unknown to her audience, had died in a German submarine. I had yet another and happier experience involving the singer in 1925 when I was living in San Diego. My husband and children joined a group of her admirers gathered on the sloping lawn of Schumann-Heink's home on Coronado Island to hear her in a Sunday afternoon concert. It was her custom to come on her balcony on Sundays when she was in residence and delight the townspeople with an hour of songs. They adored her. I did too.

Now, in Houston in the early thirties, I was to meet this grand lady, already nearly seventy years old, and talk with her. I anticipated this encounter with pleasure and, indeed, spent a happy thirty minutes with her backstage. She was cordial and gracious. In the conversation, she mentioned her great anxiety over the serious illness of a young relative in another state. "He is at death's door," were her exact words. "I am expecting the message of his death at any time." Remembering her ordeal before the Kansas City concert, I felt unusually sympathetic, and when writing the interview quoted her words about the ill relative and in passing mentioned the Kansas City happening. When the singer walked on the stage for her concert that afternoon, she prefaced it with an announcement: "The reporter on the morning paper distorted my words. I did not say I had a relative at death's door. In fact, I have no ill relative."

Bob Kelly called me to tell me of the incident "before anyone else tells you," he said.

In astonishment I asked, "Why did she say that, Bob? I quoted her verbatim." The only explanation he had was not from Madame but from a member of her staff. She was afraid the statement would offend the family in question because of their religious beliefs.

A reporter has little recourse in such cases—has only notes as opposed to the subject's words—and seldom has a witness to such interviews. I was stung that a woman I admired so much would herself resort to such distortion. But I recalled the mother giving her public full value, even as she grieved the loss of a son, and the worry she was even then suffering, even if not admitting it. "Okay," I told Bob. "Forget it. I'm tough-skinned."

The other person who called me a liar in public knew full well he was trying to throw a mistake he had made on my shoulders. It was at a National Education Association convention in Houston, and this man was the principal speaker at the Vocational Education division. He was a well-known teacher of vocational education in Washington, D.C. As school reporter for the *Post*, I covered all the main convention sessions and was sitting in the press box near enough to touch the speaker's feet. In the course of a boring speech, he made one statement I thought worthy of quoting. In the story appearing next morning with my byline, I quoted his words, delivered with emphasis.

"I hold that the purpose of an education is *not* to train a man to make a living, but to make a life worth living."

Being a well-known exponent of vocational education, he must have had afterthoughts and sought to clear himself with his peers. From the stage of the old City Auditorium the next afternoon, he held up the *Post*, read the quote and said, "Obviously, I was misquoted. I would never make such a statement. The purpose of an education is, of course, to train a man to assure his success so that he can make a life worth living."

I was looking directly at him from a distance of a few feet. He did not look at me. The other reporters in the press box laughed with me. Two weeks later, a package arrived at the *Post* addressed to me. The return address was an office building in Washington, no office number, no name. It contained what I presumed to be his apology—two pairs of pure silk hose.

As popular and talented as Helen Hayes was, and is, she was a regal put-downer of reporters when she played in *Mary Queen of Scots* in Houston in the thirties. Trying to pin her down for an interview was a frustrating experience. Again, it was the patient Bob Kelly who became the somewhat buffeted middleman. Bob set the interview at 10:00 A.M. Miss Hayes was to give her only performance in Houston that night. Local reporters were there, and the *Chronicle* reporter was accompanied by an eager cub reporter from Huntsville, a town near Houston.

We waited and waited. The star did not appear.

Bob apologized and assured us he would arrange another hour and call us. The time was set again for 3:00 P.M. This was too late for the afternoon dailies to print that day, but at three we all showed up again.

We waited — and waited. Miss Hayes didn't show. Bob was as provoked as we were. The other reporters left, but I stayed around. About five, a car drove up to the theater front and a small woman in a blue middy suit and tennis shoes jumped out and hurried into the theater. Bob started in surprise. "That's Hayes!" he exclaimed and hastened to question the car driver.

"She's been in Galveston all day," Bob told me. "I'm going to set up that interview yet!"

He called all of us and said the star would talk to us briefly immediately after the performance that night. Dutifully, after enjoying a superb performance, we gathered at the stage steps near the footlights. Presently, a young woman appeared on the empty stage and looked down at us.

"You may each ask Miss Hayes one question," she said.

We looked at each other in silence. She repeated her statement.

"You mean we are to interview Miss Hayes through you?" I asked. She nodded.

Hubert Roussel of the *Press* turned and walked away without a word. I said I had no questions for Miss Hayes and also left. Because of the disappointed young reporter from Huntsville, the *Chronicle* reporter stayed to ask a few questions but published no interview next day.

It was near midnight when I reached my *Post* desk to write the review for the morning paper. It had been an enthralling performance by a great star and cast. I said so in my review that I handed to City Editor Max Jacobs. Then I quickly wrote a flippant little story I called, "Queen Helen and the Ladies in Waiting," half expecting Jake to throw it in "File 13."

"Nice going, Bess," grinned Jake. The story appeared in the next morning's *Post,* conspicuously boxed and carrying my original headline.

Helen Hayes, whom I admire as a great artist and for the interest she has shown throughout a long life in the progress of women, is still giving of her considerable talents to an appreciative public. She probably never knew of my saucy "revenge." If she ever does, I am sure she will laugh with me about it.

During those fast-paced and satisfying days when the theaters were my most important run, I had tried and true friends backstage, always helpful, always considerate, always appreciative. I cannot thank them enough. Among these were Bob Kelly, skilled at "running interference"; Ken Douglass ("Doug"), impetuous, joking, and an optimist; Eddie Bremmer, loyal and unflappable, now deceased; and Homer McCallon, the warrior who got me fired from the movie review run but in retirement remains a friend.

Wherever you are, boys, love and appreciation.

14.

Reporting Houston

The Hogg family has long been associated with Houston and Texas. James Stephen Hogg was the first native Texan to serve as governor of the state (1891–95). His sons, Will and Mike, were developers of the beautiful River Oaks section of Houston, an area of winding streets, stately trees, walled gardens, and brilliant flowers. They lived in spacious homes there. The one Hogg daughter, the beloved "Miss Ima," and Will were known far beyond Texas' boundaries as patrons of the arts and generous philanthropists. Miss Ima and Will, never married, shared a mansion.

When Will Hogg died suddenly in 1930 while on a trip to Europe with Miss Ima, the sorrow of the city and the state was shared by many friends in many parts of the world. His body was brought back to Houston and lay in state for four days as his friends paid homage. Among these friends were Irvin S. Cobb, noted humorist, and O. O. McIntyre, a widely read syndicated columnist. They joined the funeral train in New York and rode to Houston with their friend's body.

City Editor Max Jacobs called me at home the night before the body arrived. He told me to clear my desk the next morning, get background information on Hogg's death, and meet the afternoon train.

"Get in touch with the Hoggs' business manager, H. E. Bingham, at the train and arrange for an interview with Cobb and McIntyre," he told me. "See them that night if possible, so we can run the story next morning. This story will run about five days. Make your plans to stay on it, and finally to go to Austin for the burial."

It was a choice assignment, and I knew it, challenging me to do my best. I met the train, saw the New Yorkers briefly, and arranged to meet them at Mike Hogg's residence at 7:00 P.M. I had time to rush back to the *Post,* write a lead story for the early editions, grab a sandwich and a taxi, and be at the Hogg home by seven. A maid admitted me, but when Mrs. Hogg learned I was a reporter she was less than hospitable. She had not been told of the arrangement. She informed me coldly that it was no time for strangers to intrude and suggested I leave. From the adjoining room, the men heard the conversation. At once, the rotund Cobb appeared at the door with hand outstretched and piloted me to a couch, even as he explained to his hostess. He had been a reporter himself.

It was a moving scene. The impetuous and emotional Cobb, author of many humorous books, and a much sought-after speaker on the fun circuit, wept unashamedly as he spoke of his deceased friend.

"He was one of the great human beings," he said, "always the same. In his home, in his business dealings, on these great Texas prairies and coastal plains where we lived with him in hunting lodges — wherever we were Will Hogg was the same, a friend, a *friend*. What more can one say?"

McIntyre, more reserved but obviously moved, told of the beginning of the friendship, their many meetings in New York, and of deer hunting and other sports in Texas with Hogg as their genial host.

"He was a brother, more than a friend," said Cobb as tears wet his cheeks. "I'll miss him to the end. But when it is my time to pass over that river, I know Will Hogg will have his hand outstretched saying 'Welcome Irv!'" His words did not seem pompous. They were from the heart.

Will Hogg's casket was placed on the patio of his beautiful home, facing the sloping green lawn that stretched to the tree-lined bayou. A simple funeral service was read here, and hundreds of friends and neighbors came and went silently. Miss Ima opened the parlors to all, and friends visited over coffee, lingering to speak in affection of their friend, as if in welcome to his homecoming.

On the fourth evening at sunset, the casket was placed in a rail car, and at 8:00 P.M. a coach full of friends rode with Will Hogg on his last journey to the Texas capital. Mr. Bingham had taken me beforehand to see the car, which had walls and ceiling covered with fresh red roses like those on the casket. Another brief service was held in Austin next morning, and then Will Hogg's body was laid in the family plot in the Oakwood Cemetery beside his father and mother. The plot was shadowed by a huge pecan tree that was planted by Governor Hogg himself in the early 1890s.

A tall monument stands in the center of the shrub-bordered Hogg plot. Reflecting the modest character of this prominent Texas family, only names and dates of the parents, four sons, and one daughter are engraved there. The ancient pecan tree that stood sentinel for a half-century is gone, but a younger one planted in 1967 by Miss Ima is flourishing.

Another memorable event was the electrifying news that Capt. Charles A. Lindbergh, a U.S. mail pilot, had successfully completed on May 21, 1927, a nonstop flight from New York to Paris, France, alone in a monoplane, *The Spirit of St. Louis.* In March of 1932, he paid a tragic price for his fame. His first child, Charles A. Lindbergh, Jr., was kidnapped from his crib and found dead after a few days of heartbreaking suspense. The world grieved with Charles and Anne Morrow Lindbergh.

News of the kidnapping reached the *Post* city room about 10:00 P.M. as an early "bulldog" morning edition was being printed. For the first time in my newspaper experience, I witnessed a "stop the presses" order. A new front page was made up hurriedly for a street-distributed "extra."

I was busy doing rewrites of news briefs coming over the Teletype machines, assisting the wire editor, when the news of the kidnapping came. Only a few reporters were in the city room, so I was commandeered by City Editor Jacobs to knock out rewrites, supplying the continuity needed to put the wire stories together. Jake stood behind me as I typed, snatching half-page "takes" to edit and send to the compositors to set in type.

It was nerve-wracking work, but a thrill to write this copy for the extra soon to be completed. Several of us were kept busy during the night and following days doing research and writing of the follow-up developments. This work carried no bylines for me, but the approval of my peers and editors was enough.

Other worldwide news events were reflected from time to time in my assigned stories, as local angles were found. The first sound-on-film had been released in 1927, the first all-talking picture in 1928. By the time of the Lindbergh tragedy, newsreels voiced the news, and the silent film was gone forever. During this era, the Dionne quintuplets were born in Canada (I tied local and state multiple births in a feature story); President Franklin Roosevelt broadcast his "Fireside Chats"; Hitler's rasping tirades were heard from films; Mao Tsetung started his Long March in China; noted comedian Will Rogers and pilot Wiley Post were killed in a plane crash in Alaska; King George V died in England, and after turbulent days there the new King Edward renounced his throne "for the woman I love." These were exciting days in the city room.

Jake assigned me a special project, a "Bess Scott Picture Story," which ran each Wednesday over four columns on an inside page of the *Post*. I took local events, usually humorous, and with the help of our talented photographers, Paul Peters and Bill Nottingham, illustrated them in four successive photographs. We used only enough copy to identify personalities or places. Letters to the editor were complimentary and also suggested many ideas for the picture stories.

Jake also assigned me to find, write, and have illustrated with photographs one long feature story for the Sunday edition each week. This was before the *Post* had a tabloid magazine supplement. My stories usually filled most of a regular page on Sunday. It was an enjoyable assignment but by no means an easy one. Often John Yeats, our county editor, drove me to points in our circulation area of south and southeast Texas to interview local people. Since John was also a photographer, this was an ideal association.

Brazoria and Fort Bend counties are rich in historical data and are always fertile fields for features. Among those we collaborated on was the often-told but always interesting tale of Britt Bailey, a pioneer for whom Bailey's Prairie, near Angleton, is named. A rugged pioneer, he was noted for his many feuds and hard drinking. Never able to take revenge on a certain enemy for whom he had been carrying a shotgun, it is said that on his deathbed he asked that he be buried standing up with his gun at ready and a jug of whiskey at his feet. The alleged grave of this determined man can be visited to this day. His story, doubtless with embellishments time always adds, will be talk for years to come.

The swamps of the Beaumont-Orange area of southeast Texas have long been the home for muskrats valued for their fur and for the great white egret whose silky feathers are a much desired ornament. It was my great good luck to be invited by Lutcher Stark, a nationally known Orange industrialist, to spend a day in this region in search of a feature story. With Mr. Stark as our host, a photographer, my small son Scotty, and I joined him in an outboard motorboat for an unforgettable ride on the Intracoastal Canal.

As we watched many wary muskrats flee from our intrusion and witnessed the beautiful birds perched on leafless trees or on cypress stumps, Mr. Stark told us the history of the canal, the importance of this man-made waterway and the growing fur and egret industries. He was an enthusiastic booster of this, his native territory, and had facts and figures at his fingertips.

He laughed at our misgivings as the outboard motor blades were often broken as we passed over the rough backs of alligators we could not see. After his first surprise at this, Scotty was delighted and spent most of his time trying to locate the alligators.

At one point along this route, Mr. Stark had a hunting lodge built on a man-made island. It was fully equipped, and an attendant had prepared a tasty lunch for us. An unusual and informative story and beautiful photographs recorded the day for the *Post*.

One of the passing heartaches to which reporters are subject saddened me one Sunday about this time. Reporters do not write headlines for their copy, and every page we write is subject to an editor's blue pencil. This editing is done in accordance with the timeliness of the story and space available. Since advertising gets preference over features, often a reporter's "masterpiece" is cut drastically or left out altogether. John Yeats and I had collaborated on a feature after investigating an intriguing, although highly suspect, tip that the cross which Sieur de La Salle allegedly stuck in the sand at Lavaca in 1684 to claim the area for France was still in existence and graced the spire of an ancient church building in that city.

Alas, when I opened my *Post* the next Sunday morning and crawled back in bed to check my long story, I could not find it. I supposed it had been held for another day, but later I found it in the want-ad section. The story was possibly ten inches long as printed. The only picture was a one-column view of the cross high in the air and did not even show the church! Knowing that the people in Lavaca who gave us their time and knowledge would also be looking for a long story and their pictures added to my disappointment and resentment. These hurts to a reporter's pride constitute an occupational hazard.

I hasten to say that my city editor at that time was not Max Jacobs. He was a very young son of a son of a son of a former official of the *Post*. Many of us felt that that was his only qualification.

Perhaps the most emotionally haunting assignment I ever had was to take on the telephone stories from *Post* reporters at New London, Texas, when a gas explosion at an elementary school there in March of 1937 took the lives of 394 elementary school children. Bill Gardner, Pat McNealy, and Starley Tevis were the reporters. I took story takes from them for two days and wrote them in a series that ran for several *Post* editions.

As staff changes were made, I was assigned the church run. It was not a favorite job with reporters, but since it was the custom to use only the brief notices and schedules of services brought in by the church pastors or staff members, it was not considered a hard one. Church "news" was used only once a week, on Saturdays.

I was gung-ho enough in all my work in those years to view every new assignment as a challenge. With the approval of the city desk, I began to interview pastors of different denominations about the histories and the beliefs that made the churches different. *Post* photographers would make pictures of churches, special projects, and pastors. This series ran each Saturday for thirty-two weeks, one church of each denomination featured. It was a popular series and brought us many letters, most very complimentary, a few inspired by prejudice and intolerance.

I was moonlighting a bit these days as the Houston correspondent of a Jewish religious newspaper published in New York. One day, I read a brief notice that a young rabbi of New York, Hyman Schachtel, was coming to Houston to reorganize and "modernize" Temple Beth Israel. This was one of the oldest, largest, and most prestigious synagogues in Houston and its head, the venerable Rabbi Barnston, was one of the best known men in the city. I smelled a real news story.

City Editor Jacobs gave me the go-ahead. "This may be a hornet's nest," he warned. "Go talk to Mr. Tiras; see what he knows about this." Isidore Tiras was a *Post* official in the business department and a member of Temple Beth Israel.

"Bess, this has been very hush-hush here. How did you learn about it?"

I hedged, as reporters do, about my source. "Just help me get the story, Izzy. And what is the story exactly?"

Tiras's loyalties were sorely tried. "They are holding closed meetings right now," he told me. "Everybody is pledged to secrecy. The doors are locked and guarded, especially against reporters. I go to all the night meetings, and my wife goes each day."

"They are definitely splitting the temple, turning it from an orthodox to a reformed one. People are taking sides about the reformed issues, with and against Rabbi Schachtel. Many oppose the new rabbi and the new 'Principles.'"

Isidore finally agreed to give me reports of all meetings, and the stories began to appear in the news columns of the *Post.*

Rabbi Schachtel was enraged. He called Jake and protested. He called the managing editor and others. He called me because my by-line was on the stories. He demanded I tell him where I was getting my information. He threatened to advise the whole congregation to stop subscriptions to the *Post.*

Lloyd Gregory, managing editor at that time, stopped at my desk.

"I see you got the Rabbi's goat," he said. "He called me and wanted me to fire you. Nice goin', Bess."

The Temple Beth Israel congregation adopted the new Principles, made Rabbi Barnston their Rabbi Emeritus, gave him a generous retirement pension, a new car, and paid off the mortgage on his home. The young assistant, Rabbi Robert Kahn, a highly intellectual and concerned citizen of Houston, with his followers withdrew from the temple and established Emanu-el, now one of the outstanding congregations of the South. Rabbi Schachtel still leads the congregation in a handsome temple moved from the first crowded location to a beautiful site in the suburbs. He is a brilliant man, a capable leader of devoted followers. I admire his scholarship and achievements. In his place, maybe I would have been resentful, too, but I was doing my job. We've never been friends.

All of us did moonlighting from necessity in those Depression and war years, when our always modest salaries were cut three different times. My lowest weekly check was $27.50, and it was a catastrophe when I lost my check one Saturday morning.

I stood at the center desk in the bank and made out my deposit slip in accordance with a careful budget that allowed so much to Mother for household expenses, so much to me for daily expenses, and bills. When I presented the papers at the teller's window, he asked, "Where's your check, Mrs. Scott?" I turned to the desk where I must have left it. The check was not there. "You have to watch out," the teller sympathetically admonished me. "There are people who stand around in here just waiting for this to happen."

"I endorsed it!" I exclaimed in dismay. The teller suggested that I stop payment, and I did. As I left the bank, I carefully figured in my mind how we could stretch the money I had left and the nine dollars I would get from teaching three nights in the public school. I consoled myself that with payment stopped I would eventually get my $27.50 back.

Not so. The business heads of the *Post* were not so sympathetic as our editors. This time, Mr. Tiras did not stand with me. When the head of the Henke & Pillot grocery chain, where the thief had cashed my check on a second signature, protested to the *Post,* I was told to release the check. The market was a big advertiser. I had no choice but to suffer for my carelessness.

Some solace came from an unexpected and happy break in my routine school coverage when I was sent by the *Post* to Atlantic City to cover the convention of the National Education Association that elected the Houston superintendent of schools, Dr. E. E. Oberholtzer, its president. After the convention, I made my first trip to New York City; it was my first glimpse of the city, brilliantly lighted against a winter sky from the late-evening ferry from New Jersey.

It was my good fortune to meet a friend from Dallas while in Atlantic City. He was going to New York, a city he knew well. For three days, he was an appreciated guide. He took me to hear Cab Calloway, where we had to sit behind a screen because we were not in evening dress. He took me to a little Italian restaurant with red-checked table cloths and a friendly waiter who was ecstatic when

I chose a big red apple for dessert. He took me to a hide-away bar and restaurant that was a meeting place for journalists. We filled our bowls with hot stew from big pots hanging over coals in a huge fireplace and ate at a community table covered with knife-carved autographs. Here I met Stanley Walker, native of Lampasas, Texas, then the city editor of the *New York Herald.* He later wrote the popular book *City Editor.* He returned to the family home at Lampasas and finally, preferring death to cancer, took his own life. But that night in New York, he was an affable host and regaled us with incidents of his day in the big city.

From 1931 to 1934, I taught journalism and creative writing in night school nine hours a week, and the nine extra dollars brought my income to $36.50 per week. I was talking to Superintendent E. E. Oberholtzer in his office in late August of 1934 when he asked if I had ever considered teaching journalism in high school. He explained that Milby High School did not have a journalism department, but if as many as eighteen students would sign up for journalism, I could teach the class.

On the opening day of school, it was announced that a journalism class would be offered if eighteen juniors and seniors signed up for it. When I met the group in a classroom after assembly, sixty-three students were waiting for me.

Instead of one class, I taught two, from 8:30 to 10:20 A.M., reached the *Post* at 11:00 A.M., and worked there full-time until my day's work was done—many times midnight or later. We had no union hours!

I dropped the night-school work but taught at Milby for seven years, sponsoring a semimonthly school newspaper, a student directory, and a yearbook each spring. It still gives me a feeling of satisfaction that in those years my students took many honors in the Texas Interscholastic League contests at the University of Texas, and our newspaper took top state honors two of those seven years. A few of my students have made their mark in journalism, including Bill Roberts, Houston columnist and TV personality, and Felton West, longtime *Houston Post* reporter, editor, and news columnist, later chief of the Austin Bureau. Guy Fausset went on to edit Gulf Oil publications in New York, and Ralph Cushman became a noted public-relations man in connection with the Panama Canal.

It is also gratifying to remember that on the last evening of my
night-school classes for adults, the members organized what they named
"The Scott Scribblers," later to be known as "The Houston Scribblers Club," which had an incredibly long life. Organized in 1934,
the club met weekly for forty-five years, folding in June, 1979. One
charter member, Mel Driscoll, was still attending the club in 1979.
When the club was thirty years old, the *Christian Science Monitor*
thought it worthy of a feature story. During its almost half-century
of existence, several members became published writers.

The extra work at Milby was hard but interesting. It enabled me
to send my daughter through Baylor University and my son to Texas
A&M. I stopped all the extra work in June of 1942 after my son
had joined the Navy and my daughter was married. Lila Danforth's
father had died in 1936, and she and I had pooled our resources and
built a home together in 1938. The house was something special to
us. A two-story, seven-room home with two baths, walk-in closets,
and attic and breakfast nook, it was faced with natural rock from
the Red River, its window facing all made from adobe. It seems incredible now that the whole investment including the lot amounted
to only six thousand dollars! I sold it in 1958 for fifteen thousand
dollars. In 1986, then forty-six years old, it again sold, for ninety
thousand dollars.

In 1940, it was becoming obvious that my hearing loss was increasing. Although Lila had urged me to try a hearing aid, a largely
untried invention, I had resisted. I was nearing fifty, and hated the
thought. I associated a hearing aid with old age.

Diplomatically, Lila appealed to me in a different way. My friends
were concerned about me and often were actually embarrassed for
me when I misunderstood and misconstrued things I did not hear
correctly, she argued.

So I bought an aid, a bone conductor. The battery was so large
I had to wear it strapped to my leg, hidden by a pleated or gathered
skirt. Later, I wore the battery in a special pocket under my arm and
the bone conductor instrument on my shoulder under my dress. It
was heavy and hot and produced static like the early radios. I hated
it. But I did find that it helped me to hear a speaker from a stage
and actors in plays. So I wore it for such occasions, pulling it off

in relief when the lecture or play was over. Still, the aid was helpful only to a degree.

Then a salesman persuaded me to try a new make, an air conductor. Only one whose hearing has been restored can know the astonishment and joy I experienced. It was a miracle. For the first time in my memory, I could understand a person speaking from an adjoining room, or with his or her back to me. Over the years, the instruments and batteries have grown smaller and longer lasting. I cannot wear the models made for glasses temples, or over-the-ear ones with dime-size batteries, because my hearing loss is very great. But I have learned to hide cords under curls, and small instruments under clothes. More importantly, I hear so well that people often do not know I wear an aid.

The decade of the thirties was ending, my children were in college, World War II broke out on September 1, 1939, and once again I was working in a world of ration cards and war hysteria. Many of our reporters enlisted or were drafted. A few women and older men took their places, or work was doubled. Gasoline and food rationing posed everyday problems. Mother, growing old, had gone to live with Jess's family on his Brownwood ranch and later with my oldest sister Beatrice in Blanket.

World events and tragedies were enveloping all of us. Amelia Earhart Putnam, noted aviatrix, and her copilot were mysteriously lost in the Pacific. Hitler's armies had invaded Austria in 1938, and Prime Minister Chamberlain had failed to achieve "peace in our time" by trying to appease the German dictator. Germany, Italy, and Russia were signing alliances or nonaggression treaties. In America, in the last years of the thirties, the World Fair had opened, closed, opened, and closed again. "Wrong-way Corrigan" had flown from Brooklyn to Dublin, Ireland, with no government permit, after losing his direction and flying back "the wrong way" for a time.

And so dawned 1941, a year of horrors. President Roosevelt made his famous "Four Freedoms" speech to Congress, terming freedom of worship, speech, and from want and fear essential to the peace and welfare of our country. Hitler declared a policy of genocide to "solve the Jewish question" and brought on the Holocaust. Emissaries from Japan were in Washington, talking peace, as that country

Scotty (Hubert Scott, Jr.), upon his enlistment in the Navy, Houston, 1941

launched the devastating attack on Pearl Harbor and threw the United States into World War II.

In the city rooms of the newspapers, excitement and uncertainty motivated us all. Additional work and many war-related assignments fell on everybody and new runs and new reporters were added. I was reminded of the earlier days when our daily work and lives had been completely caught up by World War I.

There was a difference—a difference that I felt. In 1918 everyone was motivated by a passion taught us from childhood—patriotism— a love of country that made the young willing to die for it and the generation of their parents willing to accept the sacrifice. Now, after more than two decades of world turmoil, disillusionment, political deceit, and national and international greed, volunteers were fewer and conscription accepted as inevitable but with little spirit of adventure.

My own nineteen-year-old son, a freshman at Texas A&M, said, "I will join the Navy. If I stay here, they will get me in the Army. I don't want to be in the Army." He served four and one-half years in every area of war. A young friend said to him when the war was over, "Scotty, I think you lacked only about eight hundred miles fighting all around the world."

My son thought a minute and said seriously, "We went to Murmansk many times, escorting troop ships and dodging submarines. We fought Japan's navy in the Aleutians and at Guadalcanal. We were in Tokyo Bay and heard Japan's surrender to MacArthur. And you know—I don't care if I never make that eight hundred miles."

He never did. At forty-eight he died of cancer.

15.

Guide, Philosopher, and Friend Lila

If it is true, quoting Cervantes in reverse, that one must eat a peck of salt with a person to prove him or her a friend, Lila Merle Danforth was the truest friend I ever had. We ate many a peck of salt from September of 1908 when I met her at Baylor Female College until March, 1942, when she died in my arms. All during those thirty-four years, she truly was, in the words of Alexander Pope, my "guide, philosopher, and friend." There is no greater proof of this than the way she welcomed me and my children and helped me get on my feet again after my marriage failed in 1927. Many times in those years we were separated, but our lives often crossed for weeks, months, and even years.

It was Lila who was always patient and sympathetic with my hearing handicap that often made me impatient, rebellious, and easily hurt. It was Lila who joined me in Dallas during World War I days, encouraged me to try my wings in Hollywood. And when I came back to a romance that died aborning, she gave me not blame but understanding and love. I knew she did not approve of my hasty marriage, but she accepted it without censure. When I returned to Houston in 1927, disillusioned, my marriage broken, and with two small children, it was Lila who welcomed us into her home and helped me financially until I got work.

She loved my children as her own. She loved Scotty, but Lila Bess was the child she never had. When she went to Washington, D.C., in 1929 as secretary to Congressman Dan Garrett, she took nine-year-old Lila Bess with her and gave her the personal care and advantages that, with night work and another child, I would have found hard to do. It was proof of our deep friendship that I felt no jealousy but was grateful that my pretty, untiring little girl had found a haven in the life of this unselfish woman.

Lila rejoiced in my joys and grieved with me in my sorrows. She knew my strengths and my weaknesses, bolstering my strengths by her confidence and, in love and without censure, forgiving me my weaknesses. Her calm, hazel eyes and firm mouth could register silent disapproval or soften with affection. In every situation, she seemed to know intuitively what to say, or to say nothing. When the sailing got rough, she was the helmsman who never panicked.

Lila was the only child of W. T. and Mollie Gardner Danforth, born in Killeen, Texas. A precocious child, she was adored by her newspaperman father, who taught her to set type by hand when she was six, her hands hardly large enough to hold a printer's stick. He passed to her his love for words and his big *Webster's Unabridged Dictionary* that was his Bible. Both were walking encyclopedias and the best spellers I ever knew.

While I was living in the Cottage Home dormitory at Baylor College where every girl worked for her room and board, Lila and her parents lived in one of the several houses that bordered the campus and were owned by the Cottage Home System and rented to families who had girls in the school. In my second and third years, my mother and I moved into the same house as the Danforths, occupying the smaller section across the hall. In December of our senior year Mrs. Danforth died after a long and painful siege of cancer. Lila gave every moment she could to her mother. The physical and emotional strain was unending, but Lila did not let it affect her grades. We burned midnight oil studying together. While I enjoyed tennis, basketball, and other outdoor activities after school hours, Lila was with her mother. But at graduation that spring, Lila was one of five seniors who tied for highest grades. We all, including the faculty members, recognized her loyalty, dedication, and strength of character.

After graduation in 1911, our paths parted. I went to Baylor University on a scholarship. Lila's father moved to a printing job in Houston, and Lila taught in schools near Houston to be close to him. In his loneliness for a home and family, her father remarried. His new wife was a young widow less than half his age and mother of a six-year-old girl. In a few months, "Dad" was calling for help. True to her nature, Lila moved to Houston. After twin boys were born prematurely and lived only hours, her father's marriage failed, and again it was Lila who filled the gap. They bought a modest home on a beautiful pecan-shaded lot. There her father died at eighty years, with "Babe" holding his hand.

Lila never married. It seemed she was destined to hold the hands of all of us—her mother, her father, myself, and in later years her namesake Lila Bess—in our times of trouble. She never made us feel she was a martyr. We knew that in every situation hers was an understanding heart, and she found contentment in helping us.

In the summer following our graduation in 1911, Lila and I had shared a vacation that we never forgot, on the Whitehead farm at Blanket, Texas. Being raised on a farm, the grain harvesting season was old to me, but Lila had never experienced it. In those days, the threshing machines were horse-operated, owned by a small crew of men that went from farm to farm and with the help of the farmer and his neighbors threshed the grain and stored it in granaries. They worked one day or more, according to the size of the harvest. This meant continuous hard work for the women, cooking for crews of six to fifteen men. The women prepared and cooked days in advance, borrowing dishes, cooking utensils, small tables to put in the yards, and even tubs for dishwashing. It became a social season, in a way, as children played and mothers cooked and served. The smell of fresh coffee from pots on wood stoves and on camp fires in the yard stays with me yet, as does the taste of fried chicken piled high on big platters, dishes of garden vegetables, washed and prepared in advance for fast cooking, not to mention the pies, cakes, and egg custards, all homemade.

Once in later years I asked my mother, "How did you manage in those hot summer days without ice?"

My practical mother went to the point: "What you never had you didn't miss."

Lila and I were eager to join in when the threshers came to our farm. We donned sunbonnets and aprons and walked down the "Big Road" a quarter of a mile to borrow dishes and flatware from Dovie Simpson, a neighbor. We swung a washtub between us. Mrs. Simpson was sitting on her front porch, hoping for a cool breeze. As she packed our tub, she told us, "I meant to ask Mrs. Whitehead if she needed me to help with the thresher, but when I heard you two big strapping gals were there I figured she didn't need me." I think she knew we "big strapping gals" were probably more in the way than being a help, but it was a good excuse.

Lila's and my friendship would grow stronger when Lila Bess was born in Denver and Lila came to visit us there. After my restless husband moved us on to California in 1923, Lila and I were not to meet again for another two years. By that time, my marriage was in trouble. When the end came, it was to Lila that my children and I went to start a new life.

In 1937, Lila joined the *Houston Post,* where I had been working for a long time. She became *Post* publisher Oveta Culp Hobby's secretary and took on the editing of the book review section. Later, in a move to infuse youth into the *Post* editorial staff, the management began to weed out older and long-standing employees. Lila was among these. Told she would be placed in the business department and would no longer edit the Book Page, she felt this was a good time for a new venture she had long wanted to try. She leased the weekly newspaper at Humble, Texas, with an option to buy at the end of the year. She was happy in this work, which was similar to what she had done as a child with her father. Lila worked in Humble from Monday through Friday, bringing her copy to Houston for linotyping on Wednesdays and returning to Houston for weekends.

Those were depression days, and I was moonlighting by teaching journalism in Milby High School and working full-time for the *Post* —a fourteen- to fifteen-hour day. My Lila Bess had married while in Baylor and graduated in 1940. In 1941, a week after the Pearl Harbor disaster, my son Scotty left Texas A&M College to join the U.S. Navy. Those were busy, stressful days and we rarely were all together. We did not dream that tragedy was near.

In mid-March, 1942, Lila suffered a severe case of bronchitis, made worse by a diabetic condition, and it grew into pneumonia. In three days she was dead. We took her to Belton and put her beside her mother and father, as was her wish.

When I returned alone to our home at midafternoon that spring day, I sought solace in our backyard, where Lila had built a rock garden bordered by flowers and guarded by a saucy cupid fountain.

I was startled to see the first spring jonquil in bloom, Lila's favorite flower. She often quoted Shakespeare's ode to the daffodil, the jonquil's sister flower, equating the two:

Daffodils
that one before the swallow dares
and takes
The winds of March with beauty

I felt the golden blossom was a message from her. I was comforted. I have been blessed beyond measure with love and loyalty of kin and friend, none given in greater measure than by my friend Lila.

16.

Affectionately, Lyndon

No matter how one views Lyndon Baines Johnson, one must agree that Lyndon was an "interesting person." I first met him in late 1930. A tall, gangling young man loped across the city room of the *Houston Post* and with surprising grace stooped over my desk. "I am Lyndon Johnson," he said. His friendly smile had no trace of the put-on reporters instinctively look for in strangers. "I am teaching speech and debate in Sam Houston High School. I understand you're the school editor and I wanted to meet you."

I was instantly wary. Another publicity hound, no doubt. As I returned his greeting, I motioned to a chair. Quickly, he wheeled it around and straddled it, leaning over its back to me.

"Mrs. Scott, I need your help. I'm going to take my boy debaters and girls' team to Austin next spring and win state championships in the Interscholastic League contests." His brown eyes laughed at his own presumption.

"Oh, you are?" I replied with open sarcasm. "Just like that?"

"Yes, ma'am." He was suddenly a little boy wanting approval. He reminded me of my own little boy, always eager for action. "Yes, ma'am, with your help."

"How can I help you, Mr. Johnson?"

"By watching our progress and reporting it." He leaned forward ingratiatingly. "We need stories in the paper."

Well. A publicity hound after all. Better tell him what's what right now. He seemed very young.

"Mr. Johnson, I hope you and your debaters have much success. Let me explain the policy of our paper. When you make *news*, we will report it. But no free publicity. There is a difference."

He was not rebuffed. He untangled his long legs from the chair and held out his hand. "It's a deal, Mrs. Scott. You just watch. We'll make news!"

Lyndon Johnson had just turned twenty-two. His Houston teaching job was his first in a large city high school, his second since graduation from Southwest Texas State Teachers College. I heard from him, all right.

He soon learned that my mother lived with me and cared for my children. By Thanksgiving, he was a favorite with my family. Mother adored him and got used to his knocking at the front screen, calling "Grandma, is there anything in the icebox?" It is well known that Lyndon genuinely loved old people. It was Mother's joy to keep something in the refrigerator for him.

My job was an exacting one, six or even seven days a week. Often while I was at work, Lyndon would bring hampers of fried chicken and take Mother and the children on picnics or to the zoo. At first, his motives were suspect with me, used to publicity seekers. He was that, all right, working to keep his debaters in the limelight. But I soon learned this high-strung, enthusiastic young man appreciated my family and found real comfort in the affection of my seventy-five-year-old mother and young Scotty, whose exuberance matched his own.

My work and my personal responsibilities made my social life almost nil. Being an attractive widow of forty, I was, even some of my friends in the media felt, fair prey for adventures—in which I had no interest. Just then, social friendships were a small part of my life. Lyndon understood this and sometimes tried to fill the void. We enjoyed an occasional dinner together in elegant surroundings with a name band. But Lyndon found it hard to unwind to the music and was an indifferent dancer. So, invariably, our conversation turned to politics, as he twirled a drink that often lasted the evening. He found me a tolerant and uncontentious listener; I found him a charming and ambitious young man. My private opinion of him was that he would go far, or burn himself out prematurely. But I appreciated beyond words his courtesies to me and his genuine affection for my little family.

His debaters? Well, it became a familiar routine for Lyndon to pick me up, often in early morning, to hear competitive debates in the high schools. Lyndon cajoled, guided, argued with, and drove his teams. He held daily sessions with them, analyzed, criticized, and praised them with stimulating intensity. He inspired in them his own ambition and love for competition and victory. They slaved for him.

At odd hours Lyndon would call me. "Can you come down a little while? I have food and coffee. I have something I want to read to you." Or, "something I want you to write for me." Or, "I have Scotty with me. I'm coaching him for his speech at the Junior Boys YMCA banquet. You must hear him!" I would steal an hour to go to his hotel home on Texas Avenue. As the food got cold and the coffee stale, Lyndon would read aloud, commenting, declaiming on political subjects and political figures.

"Joe Bailey, now there was a man! What a diplomat, what an orator! He could walk before a hostile audience and in minutes have them eating out of his hand. I'm going to be a Joe Bailey one of these days. Just listen how he did it!"

He would read the impassioned speeches of U.S. senator Joseph Weldon Bailey, a firebrand from Texas in the early 1900s, striding back and forth as he used gestures and oratorical tones for emphasis. "See? He didn't aim for the head, he aimed for the heart!"

With confidence he would say, "I'm going to be a senator one of these days. You just watch!"

I watched.

He took his boy debaters to Austin in the spring where they won the state championship. His girls' team made the finals.

I watched.

Lyndon moved on to the Washington political scene. He eventually became the Texas director of the National Youth Administration and then national director. Through this agency, set up to help needy college students, he got college jobs for my daughter in Baylor University and my son in Texas A&M. He called me from Washington as he cut red tape to arrange this.

I watched Lyndon achieve many of his goals, including the office of U.S. senator, which I am convinced was his happiest accomplishment. As his record led through the Congress to the vice-presidency and the presidency, I watched mainly from afar, as one of the little people with no influence on the larger scene.

Many years after the time I knew Lyndon as a very young teacher, my daughter Lila Bess was in Bitburg, Germany, where her husband was a captain in the U.S. Air Force. She had just lost a baby boy in the fifth month of her pregnancy because of the negligence of the base hospital staff, and I wrote to Lyndon, then a congressman in Washington. I told him how the entire American staff, including three doctors, had gone on a hunt in Belleau Woods for the weekend and left one German doctor in charge. Lila Bess had been in the hospital a few days before, and her American doctor knew she was having trouble. I was outraged. So was Lyndon. As usual, he answered my letter by telephone.

"Tell Lila Bess and George to send me a notarized letter right away about this, and I'll blow that hospital staff sky high! I've heard stories like this before from hospitals overseas, and it's got to be stopped!"

I called my daughter in Bitburg. They had already discussed reporting the matter to the American authorities, she said, but since George was in line for promotion to major they had decided against it. They had two other children and felt they had to protect their future. When I called Lyndon back, I just knew his language was burning the wires out.

From his very soul he grieved or rejoiced with his friends. He responded with total grief in 1971 when Scotty, at forty-eight, lost his battle with cancer. "My heart breaks for you. . . ." I could feel his tears. In the last year of his life, he wrote me, "I have always loved you and your family, and always will."

The Lyndon I knew was a driving, intensely ambitious man. Sensitive, complex, giving freely of himself to those he trusted, he was a man with an infinite capacity for loyalty. He also was a self-promoting man with many faults. Like all persons of vast achievements, he had bitter enemies. In his heart, he deplored this; it was his nature to crave appreciation and affection. He thirsted for knowledge, welcomed competition, and gloried in victories, but was generous in heart and spirit. Above all, he never forgot a friend.

And did we give him stories in the paper?

He made news, didn't he?

Anyone who knew Lyndon Johnson knew that he never wrote a letter if a telephone call was possible. I have a few of his letters from the time he first went to Washington in the early 1930s as secretary to Congressman Richard Cleburne, through the years of his

The author's children, Scotty and Lila Bess, Houston, 1959

presidency and retirement. In December, 1934, after certain of his plans went awry, he wrote: "Dear Bess: The receipt of your letter today made me feel like the chap who received a letter on the gallows saying it was a big mistake, two other guys were to blame. To fail is a thorn in my side."

Then on May 2, 1971, I had the last letter from my great and loyal friend before he died from a massive heart attack: "Dear, dear Bess: I think so much of you and your family, and always will. So, of course, it pleased me that you thought of me during this particular time. I, too, am grateful that I'm better and back home — blessed by such wonderful friends. Affectionately, Lyndon."

17.

Colleagues

As I recall more interesing people, one who immediately comes to mind is William W. "Bill" Gardner, who was a *Post* reporter and then city editor in the sixties and seventies. In these later years he also became director of the *Post*'s state capital news bureau in Austin. Asked to name his most embarrassing experience during his newspaper years, he told with relish how he tried to escape a dull afternoon on the criminal courts run in Houston.

"I just knew I was in for another sit-around afternoon, waiting for nothing to happen. I figured I had time to take in a nearby movie, so I walked over there. When I went back to the courthouse, I walked into great excitement. Sheriff Hill had shot his deputy Charlie Graham and then killed himself. Reporters, police, courthouse personnel, and people from the street were milling around. I got together a story for the next morning *Post*—but not one of my best."

Bill cites the New London disaster in 1937 when 394 children of the elementary school there died in a gas explosion, as his roughest assignment. With reporters Pat McNealy Barnes and Starley Tevis and photographer Jack Miller, he arrived in New London at night and worked all the next day identifying children, interviewing parents, and going to stores in the area to call in the stories. *The Post* printed an extra on the tragedy.

On the scene to try to find the cause of the explosion was E. P. Schoch, a chemistry teacher at the University of Texas. He said he was of the opinion that gas leaked from a tapped line and probably was ignited by sparks from the manual workshop. This idea was never followed up. A New York reporter in Houston on another story found a more dramatic one in New London. He took a taxi to the little town and had the driver wait there until he got his copy to New York, then taxied back to Houston.

Gardner recalled that Bill Hobby, Texas lieutenant governor in the

1980s, was just seventeen when he was made assistant on the *Post Parade Magazine*. He went to Governor Hobby, his father and final counselor. He wanted to go with a group of reporters to the Big Bend area for an article on snakes. "What kind of snakes?" asked Governor.

"Rattlesnakes, corals, and moccasins."

Governor: "Well, I don't think that is necessary." Bill knew "no" when he heard it.

Oveta Culp Hobby, who with her husband was publisher of the *Post*, kept a sharp eye on the condition of the city room, which, she often reminded reporters, was the "face" that the *Post* showed to the public. This was at the Polk and Dowling plant, an old building flanked by a railroad track and in a part of the city not noted for cleanliness. She noted reporters' desks stacked with paper and the floors covered with crushed paper rejects.

"Can't you at least get them to keep the desk stacks to about two inches?" she asked Bill Gardner.

"I try, Mrs. Hobby, but the ceiling fans and reporters' habits block my efforts."

The governor was a wise and gentle man, not easily perturbed. But the Harry Truman presidential victory really upset him.

"What do you think of the election, Governor?" a flippant reporter asked him. It was a sorry joke to the governor. He answered gruffly.

"I think I'm going to get me some better pollsters!"

Some of the *Post*'s staff had been there so long they were considered fixtures, even by themselves. One instance of this had everybody laughing about but certainly not *at* a favorite old-timer, A. E. Clarkson, *Post* business manager.

Mr. Clarkson decided to retire, and the *Post* gave him an elaborate appreciation banquet. Governor Hobby gave him the traditional gold watch, and he fairly glowed from the good wishes of dozens of his fellow workers. Next morning, to everybody's surprise, and especially to the consternation of his office staff, Mr. Clarkson showed up for work as usual!

As I recall eccentric newspaper coworkers, I think first of Hubert McWhinney. He was a brilliant and knowledgeable man, but as Gardner remembered, "He got his kicks from us reporters and was un-predictable." Once Hubert decided to live in the woods. He took over a primitive one-room log cabin. In a couple of months, he was making better Indian arrows than the Indians ever made. He made a serious study of wild flowers and adorned the billboard in our city room with samples of them, complete with detailed histories of the types and culture. If he ever neglected a *Post* assignment, we did not know it. The managing editor at one time assigned McWhinney to censor reporters' copy for grammar, composition, and clarity. And did he have a field day! He gleefully posted our glaring errors on the board with our names. If he had any friends, they could not be found the next week.

When the Wild West fever hit, McWhinney forgot his critic's role. He showed up in the city room dressed in jeans, cowboy boots, and cowboy hat and carried a rifle, which he left in the cloakroom. He kept his hat on all the time, and when he went to the water foun-tain he tried drinking from his hat brim. We eyed the cloakroom uneasily. In a couple of days, Hubert showed up with a plan for the editorial room to organize a union. Later, he left journalism and spent his final days in the woods, but no one who worked in a city room with him ever forgot Hubert McWhinney.

In the sixties the emotional civil rights issue had all newspapers, especially in the South, trying hard to find capable minority jour-nalists to add to their staffs. An ambitious black student from Texas Southern University in Houston was hired by the *Post* and added to the staff of the state editor as a "stringer," a news correspondent for a certain area. He did well and was quick to learn the city-room ver-nacular. But, he didn't escape the ribbing that was given to all be-ginners and took it with good grace. He soon was on the city news staff, on his way to department editor. Everybody was glad to see he had the right stuff.

Two very bright young women were on the *Post*'s city staff in the thirties. Pat McNealy was a quiet and reliable reporter whose com-petitors at the city desk recognized her abilities, even if they took exception to the plum assignments she received. She married her boss, city editor Ed Barnes, but the marriage did not last long. After she remarried, she left Texas and became an officer in the Women's Army Corps (WAC).

Our other female reporter was Melba Newton. If ever a person was naive, vulnerable, and street smart at the same time, it was Melba. She had expressive deep blue eyes set in an Irish "wild-rose" complexion framed by dark wavy hair. Her friendliness and her open charm brought her much attention, which she seemed to welcome, but when she found some of the men's teasing to be little short of insult, as most women would, she ignored the hurt and laughed with her colleagues.

Melba's forte was features, and her nimble mind worked overtime to find daring story ideas. One venture, however, almost became her waterloo. She went after a story of how women prisoners fared in Texas, and with the help of police friends and a tolerant judge, Melba was sentenced to thirty days on a South Texas prison farm. The plan was for her to write upon her return a day-by-day series of her experiences. The prison officials and inmates did not know of the scheme and thus treated her as a new inmate. After a few days Melba had had enough. When she tried to tell the guards and prison officials why she was there, they laughed, and some of the women inmates got rough with her. The guards finally locked her up in an old shack in a field, with insects and mice as companions. Finally, her noisy threats to have the *Post* and well-known Houston officials investigate the mistreatment that she had already seen and experienced brought results. Melba quietly returned to her desk and wrote an impressive series on the treatment of women prisoners. Letters of commendation soon restored her confidence and apparent indifference to criticism.

In the 1960s Melba traveled about in search of sensational stories for readers who appreciated such things. The grapevine later informed her old colleagues that Melba had married an Easterner with connections to New York media.

Kathleen Houston, who was not on a Houston newspaper staff at the time that I was, was one of the best "newspaper characters" in the city. This keen-minded, perceptive woman, who had in her younger days been a daring and venturesome reporter in El Paso and other cities, had printer's ink in her veins if anyone ever did. Holding a good job at the Gulf Oil Company that consisted of interviewing and writing features on Gulf people and interests throughout the South, Kathleen knew well the majority of the newspaper people in Houston and counted most of them as her loyal friends. When I visited her before her death at the age of ninety-four, she was in constant pain, but she forgot her ills and lived again the days we had shared from the twenties through the forties.

She remembered city editor Ed Barnes as a "good editor and a likeable man," one who deserved better but "dug his own grave, as the moralists say." And she continued on, telling her memories of others.

"S. P. Etheridge came to the *Post* from Beaumont and became managing editor after Lloyd Gregory. Hubert Roussel was a reporter, then amusement editor and columnist on the *Post*. He was a brilliant writer and composed some of the best columns the *Post* ever printed. He *felt* his writings and made his readers wonder, grieve, or laugh with him. His oldest son was one of the first Houston men to be lost in World War II. His account of this broke your heart, whether you had a son or not. He left the *Post* finally for the *Houston Press*.

"Do you remember Harry McCarmick, police reporter for the *Press*? A real character, Harry was. He was sent to Huntsville to cover an execution at the prison there and took his pistol with him. He got into a terrible row with the police because he would not give up his pistol. He wouldn't leave either, so finally they sent for one of the members of the Board of Pardons who lived at a Huntsville hotel to help them get rid of Harry. He was a great police reporter, but the *Press* fired him. He got a better job in Dallas."

Kathleen remembered several more of the newspapermen I also knew well: Sam Johnson, Starley Tevis, and Max Jacobs, an outstanding and especially well-liked city editor. Kathleen continued with one story about a young reporter who we both admired and who later made a real name for himself in the creative-writing world. She related how Hubert Roussel at the *Post* had hired David Westheimer, valedictorian of his class at Rice Institute, to edit the radio page after the electrical engineering graduate had reportedly been refused job placement services because he was Jewish. When offered the *Post* job, the young man said he had never written a story about anything. "Simplest thing in the world. Just put one word after another," was Roussel's reply.

That summer after his graduation David wrote the novel *Summer on the Water.* He also was becoming a popular player in the original Alley Theatre, directed by Nina Vance. David's next success was the novel *My Sweet Charlie.* Then followed the novel that brought the young writer fame and fortune, especially when it became the movie *Von Ryan's Express.*

"Lloyd Gregory was my friend, whether anybody else was or not," Kathleen Houston remembered. "He had heart. After he graduated from the University of Texas, he taught journalism. I sold the first story I ever wrote to him. Morris Frank, who became one of the most sought-after emcees and public speakers in Texas, took a correspondence course from Lloyd, who was a great teacher. He also worked on the *Austin Statesman* when I was on the *Austin American.*"

Lloyd Gregory was one of the most popular journalists of Texas. A graduate of the University of Texas and always one of its most loyal and influential alumni, Lloyd was not only a great communicator in print but was a popular emcee and featured speaker. He was sports editor of the *Post* in the late twenties and the thirties, then was managing editor into the forties. I found him an exacting managing editor, but fair and usually objective, with a great understanding and a great heart when one of his staff needed a boost and help with personal problems. He was quick to give credit and praise for work well done, and his laconic message written on the edge of a printed story, "nice goin', Bess" was an accolade to be treasured.

Lloyd knew it had not been easy for me to raise my two children from an early age on a reporter's salary and give them average comforts and advantages. Without embarrassment to me, he made me feel his encouragement. So, when a letter came to me from my nineteen-year-old son at Texas A&M the day after Pearl Harbor and I held it up and said, "I know what this is," Lloyd said, Let him go, Bess." Since he had a son the same age, I asked, "Are you going to let Lloyd go?" and he said, "I certainly am—it's *his* life." I felt he spoke sincerely and was comforted. In those days, a boy was not an adult until he was twenty-one.

Scotty came home and I signed his application to the Navy, as was his choice. In a week he was in boot camp in San Diego and served in World War II for four and a half years in both the Atlantic and Pacific.

Lloyd showed his concern for me in a more positive way. It was 1945 and I was carrying a full load of general assignments, the school board meetings and schools, churches, features, including a long one with pictures each Sunday, and special interviews. One day, Lloyd called me into his office.

"I guess you've heard through the grapevine that some of our staff are leaving and some are taking on extra work." Yes, I had heard the speculation about the changes.

"I am going to ask you take on a little more. I think you'll like it. You know many women are doing what we call 'war work' — like the women welders at the Port — and some of the women like the work and the wages so well they are staying on. I'd like for you to look up some of these women, interview them, and write a *Post* column about twice a week, featuring the women in what have been called 'men's jobs.' Think you can do that?"

"Could I do one of the columns on Sundays, with pictures, instead of the general features I've been doing?"

Lloyd liked the idea, and although I really did not want to take on this new job I remembered some of the talk going around that Mrs. Hobby was weeding out the older reporters with a view to bringing in younger ones and "pepping up" the staid old *Post*. Instinctively, I felt my job was threatened.

I did the features for a month and, in spite of everything, I enjoyed meeting the 'war' women. But I did not relish the legwork this assignment entailed. I was fifty-two years old. I was tired. I realized that the years on my toes were taking their toll. This new wartime run of interviewing and writing a column suddenly seemed too much.

Then in the manner of storybook miracles, relief came. A young friend I had known in the past as an aspiring journalist called me.

"Mrs. Scott, this is Adie Marks. Remember me?"

That I did. I had known him as a high-school boy. I had helped him place a series of sports cartoons, "Pot Shots," in the *Post* while

Adie Marks and Seymour ("Slugger") Cohen in uniform, Houston, ca. 1943–44

he was a University of Texas student. After graduating, he and a classmate, Seymour Cohen, had founded the Gulf State Advertising Agency. I had not heard much from him the last few years. Adie asked me to see him in his downtown office.

"I've had the invitation from the president," he joked as I sat before his desk. "Slugger [Seymour's nickname] was drafted two years ago. I've been exempt until now." He had a wife and small son.

"I leave in six weeks. I want you to take over this agency."

I was astonished, flattered, but not a little dismayed.

"Why, Adie, I've had no experience in an advertising agency. Years ago, I did some advertising and publicity for theaters, that's all. Anyway, why me? There must be plenty of experienced older men, or young 4-F men who would love to do this."

Adie leaned back in his desk chair. "The agency business is a peculiar setup," he explained. "The client gets well acquainted with his contact in the agency who is interested in his business and writes his advertising. In time, he doesn't care beans about the agency but trusts the account executive who works closely with him. Suppose you come in here, win the confidence of our clients, and work with them a year, three years, or however long Slugger and I are gone. Then when we come back, if we do come back, you could go down the hall, put 'Bess Scott Advertising Agency' on your door and take our accounts with you."

I saw the point. "But I wouldn't do that!"

"That's the answer," smiled Adie as we both laughed. It seemed an opportunity, and a welcome change, but I had to be honest.

"Adie, I am past fifty years old."

"So what? You look fine to me." Dear Adie. Now at retirement age himself, he still says I look fine.

"We can make it worth your while," he told me seriously. "We know newspaper salaries. We can pay you much more and will pay your gas, downtown parking, and all other expenses connected with your work. I'll be here six weeks longer to train you. Think it over and let me know soon."

I thought it over. Lila, my confidante and advisor, was gone. My family was far away. I had many friends, but none I wished to discuss this with. I loved the *Post* and had never considered leaving it until retirement. I had to make my own decision. I wanted a more relaxing job. Two days later I accepted Adie's offer. This was 1944. I was soon to learn what hard work really was!

When I told Lloyd Gregory I was leaving the *Post*, he said, "Bess, I am happy for you and relieved. I had been ordered to put you on this new port run and if it did not pan out to let you go. They are looking for *younger* reporters and editors now. I may be the next to go!" It was a shock and disillusion that hurt.

Years later, Lloyd Gregory became a victim of that tragic and mysterious illness, Alzheimer's disease, which seems often to prey on the brightest of minds. His last days were spent in that hell of oblivion.

But Kathleen Houston related to me a happier memory of Lloyd Gregory: "We always celebrated Washington's birthday which, before some smart-alec changed it, was always on February 22. One year we reporters all went to Laredo to celebrate, planning to wind up with a trip into Mexico. We had a gay time, but when we got ready to leave for Mexico, we noticed Lloyd had put his head on his hands at his table and was sound asleep. We left him. Later, he took plenty of ribbing. I remember a joke on Governor Hobby too. One day my daughter and I stopped at a paper rack on a Houston street and bought a paper. Governor had purchased one just before us and was standing near the rack with the paper in his hand. A woman came by and looked at Governor standing glumly by. She said, 'I started to get my paper off the rack, but I'll take one of yours.' His expression didn't change. He gave her his paper and took her nickel!"

I steeled myself to tell Oveta Hobby that I was leaving the *Post*. I resisted the temptation to indulge in self pity and rejected the thought that because of my association and loyalty to this pioneer paper that went back to my cub days in 1915 I deserved special consideration. Instead, I recalled that the *Post* staff—Harry Warner, Judd Mortimer Lewis, George Bailey, Ray Dudley, May Del Flagg, Lloyd Gregory, Max Jacobs, and others—had given me more than I had returned. In sincerity, I thanked Mrs. Hobby for the security, pleasure, and small triumphs I had enjoyed and her personal kindness to me, to Lila, and to my children. She accepted my comments in like spirit. When I told Governor I was leaving, he put his arm around me and said, "You are a very great lady and valued member of the *Post* family. I want you to know that if you are not happy where you are going, you can always come back to us." Although I knew I'd never go back, his words helped me to face the new challenge with mounting confidence.

It was easier to look ahead.

Epilogue

New Careers

I worked for the Gulf State Advertising Agency sixteen years. Adie Marks and Seymour Cohen had founded it in 1940, and they had operated it for two years when Seymour said: "Columbus discovered America in 1492, and in 1942 America discovered Seymour." He was drafted, and two years later Adie was called up as well.

Before he left, Adie introduced me to his father, who had offices in the same building, and told me that Mr. Marks, although he knew little about the advertising business, was a keen businessman and would be ready to advise me if I called on him. Adie paid his father one of the finest compliments I ever heard from a son.

"Captain," he said, using the affectionate title we all gave Mr. Marks, "is a gentleman. He is the finest gentleman I have ever known."

Two years later when both Adie and Seymour came home, one from the Navy and one from the Army, I had managed to hold all twelve of the agency accounts and had added one.

The Gulf State staff consisted of myself and Mary Jane, a nonchalant and unruffled secretary, eager to please but knowing no more about the complex mechanics and record-keeping of an agency than I did. In a short time, I found she was paying all bills at face value, not withholding the percentage due the agency. As Adie had suggested, we went to Captain. He set us straight and taught me mathematics I had never learned in school.

The work wasn't easy. Like everyone else during those hectic times, I worked seven days a week, and often twelve-hour days. Adie had said he hoped I could hold all the accounts, but I was not to worry if I did not. But he hoped I could hold on to their most lucrative one—Uncle Johnny Mills, a wholesale feed manufacturer of the well-known brands Eggaday, Porkaday, Feedaday, etc. He told me that Lorne Van Stone, executive vice-president and sales manager, was one of the best sales managers in the nation. He did not tell

The author, manager of the Gulf State Advertising Agency, Houston, 1957. Photograph by Harold Israel

me that he also was one of the most unpredictable and had an explosive temper.

Adie was called up sooner than he had expected, and while I had met most of the account contacts personally and all had seemed friendly and polite I had to make my first calls alone. Painfully conscious of my inexperience and my lack of knowledge of the feed products I must help him sell, I approached Mr. Van Stone with some trepidation. I had sensed his dislike of dealing with a woman when Adie introduced us, but on this first morning of confronting him alone I was determined to get along at all costs. But when, after I asked a question he evidently considered worse than stupid, he rose to his considerable height, broke a pencil in two pieces, and threw them on his desk, my own ire rose.

"Why did Adie Marks send me a blankety-blank amateur to take up my time? . . ."

"Mr. Van Stone," I interrupted as I stood up with what I hoped was dignity, "I took this agency over in an emergency and with a desire to learn and be of help, but I know Adie would not expect me to take this kind of language and acts from anybody, and I am NOT taking it." As I reached the door, I held my trembling knees taut and said, "If you want me to come back, call me. Otherwise, get yourself another agency." When out of his sight, the tears came. Adie had told me to hold this account if I lost all the others. On my first visit, I had lost it. I felt pretty low.

The next morning, Mr. Van Stone's secretary called me: "Mr. Van Stone asks you to be on the sidewalk at the south entrance to your building at noon. He will pick you up for lunch."

I hesitated. If it were my agency, I would have refused to go. It was not my agency.

The scene of the day before was not mentioned. Over a delicious lunch we talked animatedly and planned his ad campaign for the season. Years later, when I took the vacation of my life—a long tour of eight European countries along with thirty other women journalists from as many states—Van, as I called him then, gave me a hundred-dollar check and a sincere "bon voyage." By then, we were good friends, sharing a mutual respect. We are still so in our retirement years. I had learned to ignore his short-fused temper and his salty vocabulary. He had learned to accept a woman advertising consultant.

I handled the Uncle Johnny Mills account for many years and most of that time I also edited an eight-page tabloid, called *Uncle Johnny's Journal.* Eighty thousand copies, depicting success in using Uncle Johnny's feeds, were distributed in East and South Texas and western Louisiana, where the franchised dealers lived. They were put in all rural mailboxes. I was happy to be reporting again, interviewing interesting people and telling their stories.

The great variety of creative work fascinated me. Fortunately, by this time I lived alone and had no family obligations. Experienced in interviews, I enjoyed my contacts with our clients. I made new friends with shared interests. I became a member of the Houston Advertising Club and a few years later became the editor of the club bulletin *Advents,* which I edited for many years, and became an officer and a board member. It is a matter of pride that in time I became the first person to be elected a lifetime Distinguished Service member.

After a few months of farming out the Gulf State artwork, I hired a full-time artist, Jack Frost. A talented young man, he had been stricken suddenly by acute rheumatoid arthritis and walked painfully with two crutches. He could not sit, but standing, balanced by his tall table and one crutch, he turned out beautiful work. He was always cheerful, accepting his handicap bravely. He became a valuable associate. When Adie and Seymour came home from the war, they sent Jack to Denver for a major operation at a famed orthopedic hospital. This enabled him to sit down, but complications set in that necessitated another operation from which he did not recover. His death saddened us all.

It was in the mid-fifties that my national journalism sorority, Theta Sigma Phi (now Women in Communications), made it possible for me to realize a dream I had cherished since the hours I had spent as a child looking at faraway places through a stereoscope. The agency gave me a leave of absence. I accompanied thirty women journalists, only two of us from Texas, on a four-week tour of Europe. The itinerary was planned with our profession in mind. We were entertained by the London Women's Press Club and also the Women's Press Club of Paris. We interviewed Pierre Mendès-France, the French premier.

I hurriedly wrote and with my Houston librarian friend, Jimmie May Hicks, broadcast a brief message by shortwave radio from Rome to New York.

We saw an unforgettable production of the opera *Aida* in an ancient outdoor theater in Rome with rock seats carved from the hillside. We ducked our heads as we rode in the small boats into the eerie Blue Grotto of the Isle of Capri. We were serenaded by the gondoliers on Venice's streets of water. We saw the heavily guarded crown jewels in London and the Tower room where the young princes were beheaded. We walked through the ruins of Pompeii, gazed in awe at Michelangelo's Sistine Chapel ceiling, and touched the holy altar of Saint Peter at the Vatican. We enjoyed a break in our travels when we boarded an American steamer at Naples and traveled north through the Tyrrhenian Sea to Genoa.

Capping the trip for me was leaving my tour mates and spending a week with my daughter and her family on the air base at Bitburg, Germany. Then, I went to Amsterdam on the train from Luxembourg, and flew back to New York in the tail of Hurricane Carol.

Eager to forget the war and ambitious to expand their agency, Adie and Seymour added radio and television departments. The young partners quickly acquired more accounts, hired more staff, and enlarged the art department. Soon they were moving into their own new building outside the downtown area. I was assigned good accounts and assisted with copy for others, including a popular radio series.

I retired from Gulf State in 1960 at the age of seventy. The staff gave me a jolly going-away party, a new typewriter, an executive case, and an album of photographs of agency friends. This was the gift of Harold Israel, a photographer, who was counselor and friend when I was carrying on alone.

I treasure the long friendship with Adie and Seymour and their families. Jo Allesandro, a talented young drama graduate of the University of Texas, was hired to manage the radio and television department when it was added, and a few years after the war she resigned this job to become Mrs. Adie Marks. We have shared joys and sorrows over the years. Jo and Adie Marks were always at my side when I needed them most.

Adie Marks, the author, and Seymour ("Slugger") Cohen at her retirement from Gulf State Advertising Agency, Houston, 1960. Photograph by Harold Israel

After I retired from Gulf State, Scotty and his wife, whom we affectionately call Mimi, had me make my home base with them. But, when cancer took hold of my stalwart son and it became certain his case was terminal, I sought solace in work again. For another five years, I taught journalism in a Houston church school, taught a private creative-writing class for more than twenty years, and wrote communications textbooks and an informal story of my family. For a long time, teaching creative writing has been a hobby. Even now, I have a class of senior citizens at the retirement apartments where

I live. They are knowledgeable, talented writers and certainly among the interesting people I have met.

Except for a few childhood and college associates, I have found my closest friends in the communications field. I have never, during my more than seventy years in this profession, felt discriminated against because of my sex, except in the area of my paycheck. Only in very rare cases was I paid as much as men in the same or comparable job. A woman still has to work harder than a man to be even second best. I feel no bitterness now on my own account, but I do for the many talented, ambitious women of today, many of whom are still denied equality in pay and promotions.

I am grateful to all the many persons I have met along the way for their encouragement. I like people, like to talk to them, share experiences, exchange ideas. I believe the oft-quoted truth that it behooves us to listen to others, for even seemingly uninteresting people have their stories.

I enjoy challenging discussions, or just reminiscences with creative people. I feel at home with them. I especially enjoy people of the theater and value the happy days when as a charter member of the first Alley Theatre group in Houston we paid annual dues of ten cents but promoted everything from an adding machine to carpeting, furniture, seats, paint, brooms, and banners for the old warehouse we turned into the Alley, inspired by the leadership of Nina Vance. How we loved Jo Allesandro's mother, who was everywhere and everything to us in the old days! Her promotion of admissions of "a brick and a buck" inspired us all to build the attractive front to the drab building.

Journalism has truly been my life. Even outside my regular jobs, I found pleasure in reporting. For four years, I was editor of the *Texas Woman*, a state publication of the Texas Federation of Business and Professional Women of which I have been a member for fifty years. I edited *Advents* for the Houston Advertising Club for eight years; assisted the Houston Downtown Rotary Club editors during the nine years I covered the weekly luncheon club for the *Houston Post;* and over the years published many magazine articles—always happily associated with interesting people. I still do free-lance writing. But the "Great American Novel?" I do not aspire to that. I am proud to be a newspaper reporter.

I am often asked to compare newspapers of today with those of 1915 and even after World War II. This is hard to do, and my candid opinions will mark me a "square." In the early days I knew, especially from 1915 through 1920, space was available for long and sometimes "windy" stories of limited interest. We wrote more deliberately and in features were allowed a flowery vocabulary that today's reporters would find quaint and hilarious. We were required to write the news more precisely and to hold strictly to the rule of who, what, when, and where in the lead paragraphs. That has all changed. Space is at a premium in most of today's papers. News stories must be more concise. My quarrel is with construction and style. It annoys me to have to read almost to the bottom of the column to find even the "who," not to mention the "where" and the "when." Too many so-called humor columnists try too hard to be clever and become only innocuous; too many features heave and heave to bring forth a mouse.

Too many news writers slant their stories, imply opinions not actually stated. In the city-room school of my day a news reporter was just that—a reporter, not an editorial writer. Above all, too many bylines clutter the pages of today's papers. We *earned* our bylines, and they were the more treasured that they were few and far between. They were an accolade, bestowed on us by our editors for work well done. They enabled us to hold our heads high, knowing that we had the respect of our peers and were valued staff members. They almost made up for our low salaries.

Mechanical progress, of course, is superb. And of course today's paper serves today's public. A 1915 daily would be an anachronism in the 1980s.

I suppose it was inevitable that in our overcompetitive, overcombatant, overtensioned world the investigative reporter would evolve. And in most cases, to the benefit of the public. It also was inevitable that this type of "spy-reporting" would become controversial and threaten the media with censorship. To my mind, there are clearly two sides to this controversy. I deplore the current efforts of the courts to strip the press of its rights under the Constitution. I also deplore the excesses of the media in pursuing the public's "right to know," encouraged by scandal-hungry publishers and readers. I believe in fair and even fierce competition and have known the joys of a real "scoop." But I also believe in an individual's right to privacy and deplore character assassination to please a public greedy for sensational stories.

A controlled press, as has often been said, is the first step toward a dictatorship. But a self-controlled press is much to be desired. I believe strongly in the confidentiality of a reporter's news sources and applaud those reporters who have chosen jail over betraying a news source. I think the courts are following a dangerous policy in harassing a free press. But I believe also that publishers and reporters should search their motives and review their responsibilities. A good reporter, to my mind, even an "investigative" reporter, should have a conscience. I think there are those who agree, as well as those who will disagree.

I am not a crusader. So I'll get off this stump.

The years argue that I am old. I do not like the term. "Senior citizen" is even worse. I have little patience with dull retirees who talk only of their ailments, although I count myself compassionate in cases of real disappointments and sorrow. I love young people and very much want them to at least like me. Author Jane Ellen Harrison once wrote: "Old age, believe me, can be a good and pleasant time." I accept that.

To those of you who have read this book this far, stay with me. I'm thinking of writing another one, for there is no end to interesting people. It might be titled *If Life Is This Good and Pleasant at 98, Why Not Try for 100?*

Index